# Palgrave Fan Studies

## Series Editors

Louise Geddes, Adelphi University, Garden City, USA
Lincoln Geraghty, University of Portsmouth, Portsmouth, UK

This book series represents the interdisciplinary field of fan studies. It considers the different ways in which fan studies exists at the intersection of media (old and new), cultural studies, and reception studies and as a result, rethinks the production of the fields of literature, art, philosophy, theater and performance, film and television, and beyond. The series welcomes a diverse set of methodological approaches including Marxism, race theory, gender studies, affect theory, the history of print, convergence theory, digital studies, material culture, and participatory culture, as well as geographies, historical periods, and disciplines. The aim of the series is to showcase how fan studies can offer new theoretical frameworks for understanding significant artistic, literary, historical, and cultural movements, and in turn, how these innovative approaches to representing contemporary culture and media theory have expanded the Humanities.

Evangeline Aguas

# Queer Interruptions

Temporality in Femslash Fandom

Evangeline Aguas ⓘD
School of Communication
University of Technology Sydney
Sydney, NSW, Australia

This work contains media enhancements, which are displayed with a "play" icon. Material in the print book can be viewed on a mobile device by downloading the Springer Nature "More Media" app available in the major app stores. The media enhancements in the online version of the work can be accessed directly by authorized users.

ISSN 2662-2807          ISSN 2662-2815   (electronic)
Palgrave Fan Studies
ISBN 978-3-031-77024-1      ISBN 978-3-031-77025-8   (eBook)
https://doi.org/10.1007/978-3-031-77025-8

Cover credit: © oxygen/Getty Images

This Palgrave Macmillan imprint is published by the registered company Springer Nature Switzerland AG
The registered company address is: Gewerbestrasse 11, 6330 Cham, Switzerland

If disposing of this product, please recycle the paper.

*For my late mother, Patricia Capati Aguas.*

# PREFACE

This transmedia project is comprised of a book and an interactive online documentary titled, Queer Interruptions (www.queerinterruptions.com). The online documentary can be viewed on a mobile device via the QR code below, but is best viewed using a desktop browser.

View the interactive online documentary

The documentary consists of five videos, and each video has been integrated into the relevant chapters of this book through the SN More Media app. An image for each video has been placed in the text. The videos can be accessed individually by clicking on the DOI link listed in each chapter or by scanning the link with the SN More Media App.

# ACKNOWLEDGEMENTS

This research would not have been possible without the participation of the queer Clexa fan community. I would like to express my deep appreciation and thanks to the fans who took the time to complete surveys and interviews, shared the research online, and offered kind words throughout. I hope this work reflects your abundant generosity, unfailing resilience, and fierce passion for change.

Thank you to Javier Grillo-Marxuach for humbly sharing your experiences and working towards a better understanding of queer communities from creatives. Thank you to Robin Boye Danielsen, Amanda Moon, and Evan Gorman for your enthusiastic assistance while filming the interviews.

Sincere thanks go to Liz Giuffre, Greg Ferris, and Natalie Krikowa for your thoughtful mentorship, unwavering support, and camaraderie. Thank you to the editorial team at Palgrave, particularly Camille Davies and Uma Vinesh. Thank you to my family: my wife, Louise, and our child, Reyner; and George, Dennis, Almyra, Lynn, and Geoff for your love and supportive encouragement. To my friends and loved ones over the past five years—thank you.

This research was supported by an Australian Government Research Training Program Scholarship.

*Competing Interests* The author declares that they have no conflict of interest.

*Ethics Approval* This study was performed in line with the principles of the Australian National Statement on Ethical Conduct in Human

Research 2007 (Updated 2018)[1]. Approval was granted by the Human Research Ethics Committee of the University of Technology Sydney in September 2017 (UTS HREC REF NO. ETH17-1663). Additional ethics clearance was granted in November 2021 (UTS HREC REF NO. ETH21-6591), approving the use of personal correspondence with respondents. Furthermore, informed consent to participate and publish data was obtained from individual participants.

---

[1] National Statement on Ethical Conduct in Human Research 2007 (Updated 2018). The National Health and Medical Research Council, the Australian Research Council and Universities Australia. Commonwealth of Australia, Canberra.

# CONTENTS

# About the Author

Dr Evangeline Aguas (she/her) is a Lecturer in the School of Communication, University of Technology Sydney. With a decade of experience in professional film and television production, she is interested in weaving queer theory, fan studies, digital media, and ethnography with creative practice. Evangeline is interested in findings ways to queer digital space and disseminating research beyond academia through non-traditional platforms. She is also a contributor in the first-ever book exploring queerbaiting, *Queerbaiting and Fandom: Teasing Fans through Homoerotic Possibilities*, University of Iowa Press (2019) and has appeared as a panellist at the LGBTQ+ Mardi Gras Film Festival in Sydney.

# LIST OF FIGURES

# CHAPTER 1

# Introduction

FADE UP:

**EARTH. YEAR 2150.**

**INT. POLIS – COMMANDER'S CHAMBERS – NIGHT**

We open on the post-apocalyptic world of *The 100*.
LEXA, lesbian warlord, Commander of the Thirteen Clans,
and fearsome soldier, lies motionless in a pool of
blood. She and her lover, CLARKE, had just consummated
their long-simmering relationship. Instead of enjoying
post-coital bliss, Lexa is dead, accidentally struck by
a STRAY BULLET.

Clarke watches on helplessly.

BLACKNESS.

CUT TO:

**(REAL) EARTH. YEAR 2016.**

**INT. INTERNET – CLEXA FANDOM**

Twitter and Tumblr are alight.

© The Author(s), under exclusive license to Springer Nature
Switzerland AG 2025
E. Aguas, *Queer Interruptions*, Palgrave Fan Studies,
https://doi.org/10.1007/978-3-031-77025-8_1

Lexa's death triggers intense fan backlash. Fans accuse *The 100* of employing the "Bury Your Gays" trope – a trope so common it also has another name: the "Dead Lesbian Syndrome", where queer female characters are often violently and cruelly killed off.

The Twitter hashtag #LGBTFansDeserveBetter trends worldwide for consecutive days. Mainstream news gets wind of the controversy, with *Variety* publishing ''The 100' Lexa Mess: What TV, Jason Rothenberg Can Learn' (Ryan, 2016).

Fans share lists of numerous queer female characters killed on television. Their violent and ridiculous deaths are eerily similar: beheaded (Xena), arrow to the eye (Denise, *The Walking Dead*), strangled (Poussey Washington), car accident (a lot), gunshot (too many).

Images of Tara's 2002 murder in *Buffy the Vampire Slayer* flood social media. She and Lexa had matching gunshot wounds. Both were shot after having sex with their female partners. The need for bulletproof vests becomes a morbid running joke for queer female characters onscreen.

Fans are devastated. FURIOUS. Lexa's death is not just another sci-fi death. It is one fewer avenue for fans to see themselves represented onscreen. It is one more reminder that their lives are disposable; less valuable. It is one more reflection of a real-world where queer people are threatened and killed. It is one queer death too many.

BOOM. OUT.

## Time-travelling Wounds

With the death of its popular lesbian character Commander Lexa, the television series *The 100* (Morgenstein & Rothenberg, 2014–2020) became mired in accusations of queerbaiting and of exhibiting a callous indifference to its queer fan base. A year earlier, the post-apocalyptic sci-fi series had been lauded for its progressive representation of LGBTQ+ characters after featuring a same-sex kiss between Lexa and the lead character, Clarke Griffin. *MTV* had declared *The 100* "the bravest show on TV" (Murphy, 2015), while *Entertainment Weekly* reported that Clarke's bisexuality marked "a turning point" in queer media representation (Li, 2016). The three-season long romance between Clarke and Lexa was offered as proof of the series' commitment to positive LGBTQ+ storytelling, with the pair quickly gathering a devoted fan base. Fans created the portmanteau "Clexa"—with fans also adopting the name "Clexa fans"—and the couple spawned numerous social media posts and hashtags in support and anticipation of their burgeoning relationship.

Finally, mid-way through the third season on 3rd March 2016, the episode "Thirteen" featured the long-anticipated consummation of Clarke and Lexa's relationship. However, a minute after the consummation, in the very next scene, Lexa was shot dead, struck by a stray bullet meant for Clarke.

Lexa's death triggered an intense and sustained period of viewer backlash, receiving mainstream media coverage by outlets such as *Variety* (Ryan, 2016), the *BBC*, "Fans Revolt After Gay TV Character Killed Off" (Wendling, 2016), and *The Washington Post*, "TV Keeps Killing Off Lesbian Characters. The Fans of One Show Have Revolted" (Butler, 2016). Many fans took to social media to vent their frustration, with much of the criticism centred on accusations that the show employed the "Bury Your Gays" trope—also known as the "Dead Lesbian Syndrome"—where queer female characters commonly meet violent, untimely ends. Fan and media critic, Heather Hogan, shared her feelings in a post on X (Fig. 1.1).

Lexa's death transported fans backward. They were reliving the pain of yet another queer death onscreen. Their reactions were dominated by a sense of repetition—not only had this trope been employed, yet again, but Lexa's death also brought back painful experiences from their past: how they were made to relive the trauma of coming out, of staying closeted, and of previous experiences with homophobia. I was also taken back in time and felt like the scared gay child of my youth, fearful of rejection from my family and friends.

Fig. 1.1   A post on X by fan and media critic, Heather Hogan after Lexa's death in *The 100* (Hogan, 2016; Morgenstein & Rothenberg, 2014–2020)

Why did Lexa's death have such a profound impact? Hadn't we moved beyond the homophobia of the past? After all, I wasn't a closeted child anymore. I was thirty years old, proudly "out," and in a long-term relationship supported by my family and friends. By Lexa's death in 2016, same-sex marriage had been legalised in countries such as Scotland and Ireland and in several American states. There were recurring LGBTQ+ characters on successful television shows such as *Modern Family* (Levitan & Morton, 2009–2020), *Glee* (Brennan et al., 2009–2015) and Australian staple, *Neighbours* (Walsh et al., 1985–2023). It seemed like we had arrived in a new era of not merely tolerance, but acceptance. So how could Lexa's death transport me and numerous fans backward to these painful memories of being queer?

The legal advancements and growing visibility of queer lives in contemporary culture foster feelings of acceptance and inclusion. This sense of tolerance is part of a powerful and mobilising narrative on our progressive contemporary society. However, Sarah Schulman (2012) argues that this is merely "placating propaganda" used to pacify queer communities with the illusion that equality has already been achieved (p. 66). According to Tamara De Szegheo Lang (2015), the fixation with "it gets better" progress narratives serves to further bolster that propaganda:

To validate the present, there must be a past that has been overcome. For the lives of LGBTQ people today to be *better than*, the lives of LGBTQ people in the past have to have been *worse than*. For LGBTQ people today to be *happy*, LGBTQ people in the past have to have been *hopeless*. (p. 235, emphasis in original)

Narratives of progress depend on clear boundaries where a homophobic past has been overcome by a liberated present. But De Szegheo Lang argues that the neo-liberal agenda to portray queer lives as consistently improving serves to obscure the myriad ways queer people continue to be marginalised. Non-binary and transgender people have been the targets of discriminatory legislation and inflammatory moral panics in the United States. In Australia, the legalisation of same-sex marriage in 2018 has been followed by campaigns targeting transgender and gender-diverse communities, with protests and bans against drag storytime events (drag performers reading books to children).[1] While progress has been made for some members of the LGBTQ+ community—namely White, economically mobile gays and lesbians—Carrillo Rowe et al. (2015) argue that others continue to be excluded and oppressed based on race, class, and gender identity. Rather than promising a future "hospitable to all," the progress made in contemporary gay and lesbian politics merely promises that "it gets better for some" (p. 36).

Hogan's idea of "time-travelling wounds" led me to think about time: how we can experience the liberation and forward thrust of progress, and how it can be interrupted by the painful memories and backwardness of homophobia, discrimination, and alienation? The fans' time-travelling movements between past and present were more than just painful memories resurfacing: they were experiences of *temporal dislocation*—experiences of queer time.

Contemporary queer theories of temporality argue that queer people experience time differently. For example, ideas around what counts as a successful and productive life are centred around heteronormative milestones, namely marriage, reproduction, and blood lineage—otherwise called "straight time" (Edelman, 2004; Freeman, 2010; J. E. Muñoz, 2009). Queer people, however, often diverge from these straight time life paths, skipping over or reordering these milestones in haphazard ways, resulting in feelings of delay, belatedness, or aimlessness compared to their heterosexual counterparts.

Heather Love (2007) goes further to describe how queer people feel out-of-place in the present. She characterises the contemporary queer experience as "the odd situation of 'looking forward' while we are 'feeling

---

[1] See: "'Fear-mongering': Sydney council bans drag queen storytime events at heated meeting," *SBS News* (Aidone, 2024, February 29) and "Hills Shire Council rejects drag queen storytime," *Sydney Morning Herald* (Susas, 2024, February 12).

backward'" (p. 27). By "feeling backward," Love refers to the feelings associated with the pre-Stonewall era: feelings of shame, self-hatred, despair, depression, and loneliness; the feelings associated with a homophobic "bad gay past" seen in films such as *Boys Don't Cry* (Peirce, 1999) and *Brokeback Mountain* (Lee, 2005). "Feeling backward" is a lingering in the painful memories of queer history.

But rather than these painful feelings being cordoned off in the past, Love (2007) argues that these feelings persist in our liberated present—as illustrated by the fans' reactions after Lexa's death. Love argues that it is this intimacy between the suffering of the past and present that highlights "the material and structural continuities between these two eras" (p. 21). For these queer fans, the repetition of queer deaths onscreen interrupted feelings of acceptance and progress in contemporary queer lives. This blurring of temporal boundaries—of feeling backward—draws out the similarities between the queer pain of the past and that of the present. This leads us to question how much progress has been made, who is benefitting from any advancements, and who continues to be marginalised and excluded?

Love's work allows us to counter placating propaganda, encouraging us to turn backward to draw out similarities across time and highlight the ways queer people continue to be marginalised. Investigating how queer fans experience this sense of "asynchrony" and "anachronism" (Freeman, 2010, p. xxii) illustrates how the feelings of the bad gay past persist despite advancements in LGBTQ+ rights.

## FEELING BACKWARD ONSCREEN

The increasing number of queer characters onscreen[2] has also been conflated with widespread tolerance and acceptance, but the quality of those representations has not necessarily increased. The emergence of "gaystreaming" saw more LGBT specific content on mainstream U.S. cable networks, but as Eve Ng (2013) explains, racial and sexual diversity were overlooked in favour of more (homo)normative representation.

---

[2] GLAAD's *Where Are We on TV* (2022) report noted a record high 11.9% of U.S. series regular characters were LGBTQ+ . Similarly, Screen Australia's *Seeing Ourselves 2* (2023) reported a 2.9% increase in the number of LGBTQ+ characters on Australian screens.

Diversity was diluted for more "gender-conforming behaviors, normative family structures, and consumption and middle-class taste cultures" (p. 261). The faux-diversity of more queer characters was merely a case of "plastic representation," where "the degree of diversity became synonymous with the quantity of difference rather than with the dimensionality of those performances" (Warner, 2017, p. 33). This was not a new liberatory age for gay and lesbian viewers—just increased commercial viability and another group objectified. The new-found profitability of LGBT content relied on a form of depoliticised queerness more palatable (and less defiant) on mainstream networks.

In a cruel twist, more queer characters has also led to more queer death onscreen. The annual *Where We Are on TV* report published by the LGBTQ+ media advocacy organisation, GLAAD (2017) noted that 2016 was "a very deadly year for queer female characters" on American broadcast and cable networks, with more than 25 characters killed since the beginning of 2016 (p. 3). The non-profit organisation LGBT Fans Deserve Better also collated statistics on the percentage of dead queer female characters between 1976 and 2016, and found that high profile networks such as HBO, NBC, SYFY, and FX had particularly high rates of queer female deaths (LGBT Fans Deserve Better, 2017). The report highlighted that a disproportionately large percentage of characters killed onscreen were lesbian or bisexual women, with 61 out of 288 considered, or 21% of all represented. The queer online magazine, *Autostraddle* (Riese, 2023) also compiled a list of the victims of this trope from 1976 to the present, and as of November 2023, stands at 235 lesbian or bisexual female characters killed onscreen.

Although there is no evidence to suggest that these characters were targeted due to their queerness, there is considerable overlap between disposable characters and those who are queer and female. While Navar-Gill and Stanfill (2018) acknowledge that "it is untenable to exempt certain characters from jeopardy simply because they are from marginalised populations" (p. 95), the ongoing trend towards queer characters dying onscreen points to a "system of representational oppression" (p. 97). A lack of diversity in writers' rooms and at studio executive levels, alongside a perceived lack of interest in and profitability of queer stories has relegated queer characters to the margins as disposable and secondary players.

Queer erasure is also seen in the cancellation of television shows featuring queer characters. The most recent GLAAD report (2023) highlights that almost a third of LGBTQ+ characters appearing over the past year will not return to screens (Chilton, 2023). Seen as another iteration of the Bury Your Gays trope, "Cancel Your Gays" has seen the cancellation of eight shows with queer female leads on U.S television in 2022: The CW's *Batwoman*, Netflix's *First Kill*, and HBO's *Gentleman Jack*, to name a few (Anderson, 2023; Piccoli, 2023).

The Amazon Prime series, *A League of Their Own* (Babbit et al., 2022) featured multiple queer female characters and had been renewed for a truncated second season, only to be cancelled soon afterwards in August 2023. Showrunner and writer, Will Graham consoled disappointed fans on X (formerly Twitter):

> Most of us grew up feeling invisible, and as we gain strength, the predictable backlash forces are trying their hardest to get us to go back underground. In case anyone needs to hear it: You are not small, niche, modest, off-putting or marginal, and neither are your stories. You are multitudes, you are building, and your stories are universal. You are the most rapidly growing audience and consumer group in this country. You are powerful. You are the future, and ultimately the people who don't recognize your importance now will feel (sic) be clamoring to catch up in a few years. (Graham, 2023)

The cancellation of LGBTQ+ inclusive shows tells queer audiences that they are not valued and that their stories do not deserve space in the mainstream. The removal of these shows from the catalogues of streaming services after cancellation also erases queer media from popular culture archives. It is not just an issue of cancellation, but also of access. While cancellation ensures that queer characters are spared untimely deaths, their stories remain untold, and their cultural value to audiences dismissed by screen industries. Despite the normalising agenda of contemporary screen media, queer representation remains bound by capitalist and heteronormative structures that depoliticise, deradicalise, and eliminate queerness onscreen.

Queer death onscreen does not occur in a vacuum—it speaks to the systemic oppression of queer people and how this has been translated into a long history of marginalisation and censorship in screen media. And while there have been advancements in LGBTQ+ rights, progress does not follow a linear path from a homophobic past to a liberated present. Rather, queer audiences are left to navigate between visibility and erasure; assimilation and alienation; dissidence and depoliticisation. How fans move between and inhabit these polarities reveals their shifting temporal movements: queer fans find themselves caught between the forward thrust of progress and the backwardness of screen tropes; reliving the past and feeling out-of-place in the present.

This project focuses on the queer femslash[3] fans of *The 100*'s same-sex couple, Clarke and Lexa—the "Clexa" fans—and explores how they experience queer temporalities. By framing the fans' experiences as temporal movements—as feeling out-of-sync, as delay, as anachronism—we can achieve a more nuanced and complex view of the passage of progress. In what ways do they feel out-of-sync or delayed compared to their heterosexual peers? In what ways do they feel backward while LGBTQ+ rights advance forward? How is time structured as White Time and what impact does this have on queer fans of colour? Exploring the fans' experiences of queer time allows us to question the extent of liberation: which sectors of the LGBTQ+ community are accepted (or perhaps merely protected) and who continues to be marginalised?

This project also considers the tension between abstract theory and materiality. Queer theory has been criticised as being too abstract to engage in the realities of everyday queer experience (Browne & Nash, 2010). Through an ethnographic approach and accompanying online documentary, I uncover the different facets of queer temporalities in lived experience: how do delay, belatedness, and anachronism manifest in our emotional lives? How do these fans experience delay in different ways? What does feeling backward look like? Through documentary video and website design, these intangible queer temporalities are made visible, material, and transmissible.

## A Queer Transmedia Project

This transmedia project is comprised of a book and an online documentary titled, Queer Interruptions (www.queerinterruptions.com) (Aguas, 2021). Each work offers different and complementary experiences. The book has a traditional structure, whereas the online documentary uses the

---

[3] Femslash refers to romantic or sexual pairings between two female characters, often written as "f/f."

affordances of website media to express queer temporalities in its form, design, and user experience. Both works explore theory, materiality, and emotionality. The boundaries between these works and categories blur and bend, offering multiple points of entry for different readers, users, and perspectives. The website can be viewed on a mobile or tablet device via the QR code below, but is best viewed using a desktop browser (Fig. 1.2).

The transmedia components can also be viewed in tandem. The documentary consists of five videos, and each video has been integrated into the relevant chapters of this book through the SN More Media app. An image for each video has been placed in the text; simply click on the DOI link provided under the Supplementary Information section of each chapter or scan the link with the SN More Media App to view the video on your mobile device.

The following chapters provide insight into the shifting, contradictory, and dynamic experiences of contemporary queerness using Clexa fans as a case study. Chapter 2, "The Ideal Fan vs The Rest of Us," looks at the shifting position of fans in contemporary culture, where changes in digital social and screen media industries have given some fans increasing cultural power while others remain on the margins. This section also addresses the dominant Whiteness of existing fan studies, positioning the project as part of a growing body of scholarship mitigating the invisibility of queer fans of colour.

Chapter 3, "A Queer Ethnography," details the methodologies employed and explains the processes used in participant recruitment. It explains how research participants were pre-qualified through a screening process to find respondents whose experiences could be linked to conceptions of queer time, and how stimulus material was used during the

**Fig. 1.2** Scan the QR code with your mobile device to view the online documentary

in-depth interviews to assist in extending and elaborating on abstract discussions of time.

In Chapter 4, "Queer Disorientations: Delay and Extended Adolescence," I examine how fans inhabit queer time: how do they experience a sense of being out-of-sync, delayed or in stasis? I discuss the gendered and racialised heteronormativities that continue to marginalise queer people, where fans reveal persistent feelings of delay and belatedness and of having to "catch up" to their heterosexual counterparts. Their experiences of delay are then paralleled with their experiences as fans, illustrating how some fans continue to be stigmatised and framed as delayed, arrested in their development, and deviant. However, rather than fulfilling the negative connotations of these stereotypes, the delayed and meandering adulthoods of queer fans are instead experienced as opportunities for liberation and alternative life rhythms.

In Chapter 5, "Queer Death Onscreen: Anachronism, Bad Feelings, and Melancholia," I discuss how fans experience a lingering in the past and a sense of feeling backward. Fans recount how Lexa's death on *The 100* (Morgenstein & Rothenberg, 2014–2020) caused them to relive past homophobic experiences, where her onscreen demise resonated with their previous experiences of rejection, erasure, and fear of violence. This chapter explores these time-travelling wounds, specifically how Lexa's death could transport fans to painful personal histories. An examination of the fans' backward movements identifies how the past is in constant engagement with the present—interrogating the felt experience of anachronism. For queer fans of colour, these backward feelings are also examples of a queer racialised melancholia and serve to highlight continuing injustices and how colonial legacies persist in the present.

In Chapter 6, "Queer Interruptions: A Fan Gift and Queer Archive of Feelings," I discuss how the interactive online documentary genre has shaped the creative component and how the genre can be a productive intervention in social justice issues. I also detail how the online documentary participates in the gift economy of fandom and contributes to an online fan culture marked by education, social justice, and solidarity-building. As a queer, visual archive of feelings, Queer Interruptions expresses the temporal fluidity, transience, and intangibility of the fans' emotional lives.

The concluding chapter of this work, "Life After Death (On Repeat)" discusses the ongoing use of the Bury Your Gays trope in 2023, highlighting the continuing relevance of this research. This chapter recounts how queer fans continue to grapple with the temporal oscillations between visibility and erasure; assimilation and alienation. Although perpetual backwardness, anachronism, and melancholia can bear negative connotations, they can also be catalysts for meaningful social action and political change. This chapter reiterates how inhabiting queer temporalities—"'looking forward' while we are 'feeling backward'"(Love, 2007, p. 27)—allows us to weave threads between the past and present, not only highlighting the progress made but also the inadequacies that continue to oppress and marginalise queer people.

## A Few Words of Clarification

This study had initially focused on self-identifying queer female fans but as the research progressed, the scope had expanded and narrowed in various ways. The initial call-outs were posted on social media and asked fans to opt-in. The majority of respondents were cisgender women; no transgender women had opted-in to the research. While I made sure to highlight that self-identification was an important qualifier, in hindsight, the research call-outs could have been made more inclusive and welcoming for transgender participants, who have historically been neglected within existing fan scholarship (Clyde, 2021; Duggan, 2021).

Despite the limitations around transgender perspectives, the scope was expanded to include non-binary identities. After the interviews had been conducted and during data analysis, several participants came out as non-binary or genderqueer (here, I use those two terms interchangeably). They did not withdraw from the research and their responses were included in this book to demonstrate continuities between the fans' a/gendered experiences. For each participant in this book, I have included their pronouns alongside other identifying information. The online documentary website also lists the pronouns of each participant featured in the videos and text quotes.

Although the book analyses the experience of one genderqueer participant and the online documentary features three genderqueer participants, it does not constitute the bulk of the analysis. The complexity of transgender, non-binary, and gender-diverse experiences warrants in-depth study beyond the scope of this project. I acknowledge that retaining a focus on self-identifying queer female fans risks reinforcing "binarizing labelling" and contributing to the erasure of gender-diverse fans (Duggan, 2021, p. 6). Despite this, I believe that queer female and genderqueer fans diverge from straight time in overlapping ways, preserving the capacity of this research to provide insight into the state of contemporary queerness (and of feeling backward) today. In accepting the limitations of this research, I nonetheless hope to illuminate possible points of intersection and identify areas for future research.

The use of the term "queer female" may also be problematic. Queer theory's primary project is to critique heteronormative ideologies, highlighting the social construction of seemingly innate identity categories. It disrupts sexual and gender binaries, instead emphasising ambiguity, fluidity, and indefinability. Using the term "queer female" and marking boundaries according to gender and sexual identity seems at odds with queer theory's ethos of anti-essentialism, plurality, and indeterminacy. But my use of the term is designed to counter the characterisation of queer theory as gender-neutral. Suzanna Walters (1996) argues against ideas of queerness as "somehow beyond gender, a vision of a sort of transcendent polymorphous perversity" which, rather than transcending gender, works to marginalise gender, women, and lesbians (p. 844). She argues that, instead of conceiving a gender-neutral subject, queer theory instead constructs a "universal gay male subject, as its implicit referent" (p. 846). This conception of queerness "erases lesbian specificity" and the impact of gender in women's lived experiences (p. 843). This tension points to one of the contradictions of queer theory: while it rejects these rigid identity politics in the abstract, the lived experiences of queer people show that these identity politics are relevant to how some achieve a sense of belonging and are often drawn upon to justify political activism (Oleksiak & Tiffe, 2015). In *Queer Praxis*, Kimberlee Pérez reflects on this ironic position: that while queerness allows her "to move beyond, through [and] between" the cracks and spaces of essentialism, she is also "not ready to give up" identity politics or essentialist arguments (Tiffe et al., 2015, p. 218). I use the term here to acknowledge its significance in the lived realities of my participants and to give specificity and context to their experiences.

I also draw on J. E. Muñoz's use of "queer" to refer to a mode of being and thinking, which is "the force of a kind of queer doing" (2009, p. 84). To be "queer" is to adopt a radical political opposition to normative conceptions of gender, sexuality, identity, and social order. I use the term here to emphasise how these fans exist outside of heteronormativities and how they challenge social norms. Their actions and experiences speak to the transgressive, resistant, and resilient qualities of queer praxis.

Furthermore, I do not argue that all queer people experience feelings of backwardness, delay, and alienation. The legalisation of same-sex marriage and the extension of adoption and parenting rights to same-sex couples in countries such as the United States and Australia has meant that not all gay, lesbian, and transgender people live opposite lives to their heterosexual peers (Freeman, 2010; Halberstam, 2005). Rather, this research focuses on the ways that queer people, particularly queer people of colour, continue to be marginalised despite these advancements. To this end, participants were pre-qualified and screened to identify those who continue to experience alienation and backwardness. Stimulus cards were also used during interviews to make abstract concepts such as queer temporalities more accessible and perceivable for respondents (this is discussed further in Chapter 3). The interviews were also conducted with due diligence following the University of Technology Sydney's ethics guidelines, approval numbers UTS HREC REF NO. ETH17-1663 and UTS HREC REF NO. ETH21-6591.

## References

Aguas, E. (2021, July). *Queer interruptions*. https://queerinterruptions.com

Aidone, D. (2024, February 29). 'Fear-mongering': Sydney council bans drag queen storytime events at heated meeting. SBS News. https://www.sbs.com.au/news/article/fear-mongering-council-bans-drag-queen-storytime-events-at-heated-meeting/t0n9vslf8

Anderson, D. (2023, June 22). Lesbian TV shows 'targeted by cancellations'. MOJO News. https://www.mojonews.com.au/gender-and-sexuality/lesbian-tv-shows-targeted-by-cancellations

Babbit, J., Graham, W., Jacobson, A., Tedros Reff, D., & Wierengo, H. (Executive Producers). (2022). *A League of Their Own* [TV series]. Amazon Studios; Field Trip Productions; Sony Pictures Television.

Brennan, I., Buecker, B., Di Loreto, D., Falchuk, B., & Murphy, R. (Executive Producers). (2009–2015). *Glee* [TV series]. Brad Falchuk Teley-Vision; Ryan Murphy Productions; 20th Century Fox Television.

Browne, K., & Nash, C. J. (Eds.). (2010). *Queer methods and methodologies: Intersecting queer theories and social science research*. Ashgate Publishing. https://doi.org/10.4324/9781315603223-1

Butler, B. (2016, April 4). TV keeps killing off lesbian characters. The fans of one show have revolted. *The Washington Post*. https://www.washingtonpost.com/news/arts-and-entertainment/wp/2016/04/04/tv-keeps-killing-off-lesbian-characters-the-fans-of-one-show-have-revolted/?utm_term=.8c6be4eb99df

Carrillo Rowe, A., Tiffe, R., Goltz, D. B., Zingsheim, J., Bagley, M., & Malhotra, S. (2015). Queer love: Queering coalitional politics. In D. B. Goltz & J. Zingsheim (Eds.), *Queer praxis: Questions for LGBTQ worldmaking* (pp. 123–139). Peter Lang Publishing. https://doi.org/10.3726/978-1-4539-1439-7

Chilton, L. (2023, March 21). Almost a third of queer TV characters will disappear from screens next year, report finds. *The Independent UK*. https://www.independent.co.uk/arts-entertainment/tv/news/lgbt-cha racters-queer-glaad-tv-report-b2305121.html

Clyde, D. (2021). Flying on borrowed feathers: Identity formation among gender-variant anime fans in the U.S., *Feminist Media Studies*, *21*(6), 1050–1053. https://doi.org/10.1080/14680777.2021.1959371

De Szegheo Lang, T. (2015). The demand to progress: Critical nostalgia in LGBTQ cultural memory. *Journal of Lesbian Studies*, *19*(2), 230–248. https://doi.org/10.1080/10894160.2015.970976

Duggan, J. (2021). "Worlds…[of] contingent possibilities": Genderqueer and trans adolescents reading fan fiction. *Television and New Media*. https://doi. org/10.1177/15274764211016305

Edelman, L. (2004). *No future: Queer theory and the death drive*. Duke University Press.

Freeman, E. (2010). Time binds: Queer temporalities, queer histories. *Duke University Press*. https://doi.org/10.1215/9780822393184

GLAAD Media Institute. (2017). *Where we are on TV '16-'17*. GLAAD. https:// glaad.org/publications/whereweareontv16/

GLAAD Media Institute. (2022). *Where we are on TV 2021–2022*. GLAAD. https://glaad.org/whereweareontv21

GLAAD Media Institute. (2023). *Where we are on TV 2022–2023*. GLAAD. https://glaad.org/whereweareontv22

Graham, W. [@WillWGraham]. (2023, August 24). *Most of us grew up feeling invisible, and as we gain strength, the predictable backlash forces are trying their hardest*. X. https://twitter.com/willwgraham/status/169439946848 8290609?s=12&t=P9qVV0-06XlAKfpvzbYYAg

Halberstam, J. (2005). In a queer time and place: Transgender bodies, subcultural lives. *New York University Press*. https://doi.org/10.1007/s10508-007-9224-x

Hogan, H. [@theheatherhogan]. (2016, March 4). *Straight TV writers will never understand how they can inflict time-traveling wounds that hurt us as scared gay children all*. X. https://web.archive.org/web/20190727050802/ https://twitter.com/theheatherhogan/status/705814487786512384

Lee, A. (Director). (2005). *Brokeback mountain*. [Film]. Focus Features; River Road Entertainment; Alberta Film Entertainment; Good Machine.

Levitan, S., & Morton, J. (Executive Producers). (2009–2020). *Modern Family* [TV series]. Levitan / Lloyd; 20th Century Fox Television; Steven Levitan Productions; Picador Productions.

LGBT Fans Deserve Better. (2017). *Lesbian and bisexual women on TV: A look at the state of representation from 1976–2016*. https://lgbtfansdb.com/editor ial/lesbian-bisexual-women-tv-look-state-representation-1976-2016

Li, S. (2016, February 17). *The 100*: Why defining Clarke's bisexuality marked a "turning point" for the CW series. *Entertainment Weekly*. http://ew.com/article/2016/02/17/the-100-clarke-bisexuality/

Love, H. (2007). *Feeling backward: Loss and the politics of queer history*. Harvard University Press.

Morgenstein, L., & Rothenberg, J. (Executive Producers). (2014–2020). *The 100* [TV series]. Alloy Entertainment; CBS Television Studios; Warner Bros. Television.

Muñoz, J. E. (2009). *Cruising utopia: The then and there of queer futurity*. New York University Press.

Murphy, S. (2015, February 26). *"The 100" just became the bravest show on TV with its badass LGBT kiss*. MTV. http://www.mtv.com/news/2090716/the-100-clarke-lexa-bisexual-kiss/

Navar-Gill, A., & Stanfill, M. (2018). "We shouldn't have to trend to make you listen": Queer fan hashtag campaigns as production interventions. *Journal of Film and Video, 70*(3–4), 85–100. https://doi.org/10.5406/jfilmvideo.70.3-4.0085

Ng, E. (2013). A "'post-gay'" era? Media gaystreaming, homonormativity, and the politics of LGBT integration. *Communication, Culture & Critique, 6*, 258–283. https://doi.org/10.1111/cccr.12013

Oleksiak, T., & Tiffe, R. (2015). Queering the ear: Listening queerly to anger and decorum. In D. B. Goltz & J. Zingsheim (Eds.), *Queer praxis: Questions for LGBTQ worldmaking* (pp. 187–191). Peter Lang Publishing. https://doi.org/10.4324/9781315612959-19

Peirce, K. (Director). (1999). *Boys don't cry*. [Film]. Searchlight Pictures; The Independent Film Channel Productions; Killer Films; Hart Sharp Entertainment.

Piccoli, D. (2023, January 17). *Queer fans and the fight against "Cancel your gays"*. News Is Out. https://newsisout.com/2023/01/queer-fans-and-the-fight-against-cancel-your-gays/

Riese. (2023, February 27). All 235 dead lesbian and bisexual characters on TV, and how they died. *Autostraddle*. Retrieved November 18, 2023, from https://www.autostraddle.com/all-65-dead-lesbian-and-bisexual-characters-on-tv-and-how-they-died-312315/

Rubel Kuzui, F., Kuzui, K., Whedon, J., Berman, G., Gallin, S., & Noxon, M. (Executive Producers). (1997–2003). *Buffy the Vampire Slayer*. [TV series]. Mutant Enemy; Kuzui Enterprises; Sandollar Television; 20th Century Fox Television.

Ryan, M. (2016, March 14). "The 100" Lexa mess: What TV, Jason Rothenberg can learn. *Variety*. http://variety.com/2016/tv/opinion/the-100-lexa-jason-rothenberg-1201729110/

Schulman, S. (2012). *The gentrification of the mind: Witness to a lost imagination*. University of California Press.

Screen Australia. (2023, April). *Seeing ourselves 2: Diversity, equity and inclusion in Australian TV drama*. https://www.screenaustralia.gov.au/fact-finders/reports-and-key-issues/reports-and-discussion-papers/seeing-ourselves-2

Susas, J. (2024, February 12). Hills Shire Council rejects drag queen storytime. *Sydney Morning Herald*. https://www.smh.com.au/national/nsw/hills-shire-council-rejects-drag-queen-storytime-20240212-p5f47w.html

Tiffe, R., Bagley, M., Zingsheim, J., Pérez, K., & Goltz, D. B. (2016). Queer love: Futurity and potentiality. In D. B. Goltz & J. Zingsheim (Eds.), *Queer praxis: Questions for LGBTQ worldmaking* (pp. 215–229). Peter Lang Publishing. https://doi.org/10.3726/978-1-4539-1439-7

Walsh, S., Herbison, J., Battye, D., Pellizzeri, R., Maier, R., Jasek R., Watson, R., & Bower, S. (Executive Producers). (1985–2023). *Neighbours* [TV series]. Grundy Television Australia; Amazon Studios; Grundy Television Productions; JM Agency; The Grundy Organisation.

Walters, S. D. (1996). From here to queer: Radical feminism, postmodernism, and the lesbian menace (or, why can't a woman be more like a fag?). *Signs: Journal Of Women In Culture & Society*, 21(4), 830–869. https://doi.org/10.1086/495123

Warner, K. (2017). In the time of plastic representation. *Film Quarterly*, 71(2), 32–37. https://www.jstor.org/stable/26413860

Wendling, M. (2016, March 11). *Fans revolt after gay TV character killed off*. BBC News. http://www.bbc.com/news/blogs-trending-35786382

# CHAPTER 2

# The Ideal Fan vs The Rest of Us

Screaming, hysterical teenage girls greeting The Beatles. A nerdy, forty-year-old virgin with shelves of collectibles. While these fans certainly still exist, the stigmatised basement-dweller stereotype has changed. With the movement towards digital media and increased interactions between creators and audiences, fans and fan practices have become normalised and commodified. Fans have found themselves in a position of relative cultural power, where their attention and labour are increasingly lucrative and sought after. However, queer fans and fans of colour remain excluded from this shift, questioning the extent of the mainstreaming of fandom.

Early fan scholarship challenged negative stereotypes of fandom as a pathology, instead portraying fandom as legitimate subcultural participation (Bacon-Smith, 1992; Fiske, 1992; Jenkins, 1992). Rather than being maligned as "cultural dupes, social misfits, and mindless consumers," fans constituted an interpretive community and were "active participants in the construction and circulation of textual meanings" (Jenkins, 1992, pp. 23–24). However, Jenkins argued that there were limits to their active participation as they remained excluded from commercial cultural production and had "only the most limited resources with which to influence [the] entertainment industry's decisions" (1992, p. 27). Fast forward to the advent of the internet, where the rise of digital media blurred the boundaries between consumers and creators and assisted in normalising models of fan participation (Jenkins, 2006; see also Gray et al., 2007;

E. Aguas, *Queer Interruptions*, Palgrave Fan Studies, https://doi.org/10.1007/978-3-031-77025-8_2

19

Zwaan et al., 2014). Convergence culture and the interdependence of digital media systems allowed for greater dissemination of user-generated content and increased interaction between producers and consumers. But rather than ushering in a new era of democratic media participation, Jenkins (2006) argued that these shifts were economically driven and that the producer–consumer relationship fluctuated between commodification, exploitation, and "tactical collaboration" (p. 250). As media industries have embraced convergence to their own advantages, models of fan consumption have become the ideal, where "fannish modes of sharing and spreading interest get rebranded as viral marketing" (Busse, 2015, p. 112). Zwaan et al. (2014) also insist that the increasing use of mobile technology has led to a climate where the fan model of participatory culture is "no longer a niche phenomenon, but has become the new normative standard" such that, now, "everyone is a fan" (p. 2). Likes, reposts, hashtags, memes, and binge-watching have become monetised engagements so commonplace that non-participation renders you a technophobe, luddite, or just plain boring.

While there has been a growing acceptance of fans and fan practices, claiming that fandom is mainstream masks the ways some fans continue to be relegated to the margins. Contemporary scholarship has identified how the ideal fan is conceptualised as White, male and straight, whereas problematic or negative fans are women, people of colour and queer people (Busse, 2015; Pande, 2020b; Stanfill, 2019a). Traditionally male-dominated fan activities and attachments tend to be affirmational, reinforcing the authority and intended meanings of the original work, with greater success of acknowledgement and renumeration. On the other hand, female-dominated fan activities tend to rework the original text to make or uncover new meanings, challenging authorial intent and avoiding (or being deemed unworthy of) monetisation. Mel Stanfill (2019a) writes that feminised fan practices such as fan fiction and vidding are marked by a "refusal of monetization, resistance to authorial control, and often touchy-feely subject matter" that renders them undesirable (and unprofitable) to media companies (p. 32). There is clearly a "right way" for fans to interact with media, where those deemed immature, emotional, obsessive, and feminine are not embraced by the mainstream (Busse, 2015; Stanfill, 2013).

The overwhelming number of White gatekeepers of mainstream Western media, the lack of multi-dimensional characters of colour, and the prevailing Whiteness of fan spaces have also made fandom unwelcoming for fans of colour (Pande, 2020b; Wanzo, 2015). Kristen Warner (2015) explains that fandom is conceptualised as a "non-identity-specific-yet-common-interests phenomenon" which downplays the relevance of race, class, and gender to fan identity and experience (p. 34). However, the non-specific identity is White by default, invisibilising fans of colour. The default Whiteness of fandom also constructs Whiteness as neutral, rather than as a racialised identity (Pande, 2020a; Stanfill, 2018). If Whiteness remains an unspoken identity marker, then its role in shaping fandom dynamics and experiences also remains unspoken. Discussions of race/racism are seen as irrelevant or even ruinous to the experience of fandom. Pop culture commentator, Stitch (2021a) argues that if fandom is seen as escapist, it only provides relief for White fans, whose protective bubble safeguards them from the racial politics of the outside world. Fans who highlight racial harassment towards actors of colour or call out racism from fellow fans are labelled "fandom killjoys" and are seen as the root of fandom conflict or as anti-fans (Pande, 2020b, p. 17). Stitch (2021b) also argues that fandom breeds misogynoir, where Black women are subjected to intense harassment as "people see them as 'infringing' on these nerdy spaces—and it's not just dudebros doing the harassment." Mainstream fandom continues to centre Whiteness not only through an active hostility towards fans of colour, but also in its refusal to acknowledge the default Whiteness of fandom itself. As Warner (2015) writes, "The stark reality is that the only people who are allowed to be visible within fandom and imagined to be fans by the media industries are White men and women" (p. 33).

Industry attention to "ideal fans" is also mirrored by a dominant focus on White male and female fans of Western media in fan studies scholarship. Femslash fan communities have largely been overlooked in existing research, but a growing number of studies are mitigating this invisibility. These studies often frame femslash fandom as subversive and inclusive, though it is clear that the field remains constrained by racial power structures that continue to push some fans to the margins.

The subversive potential of femslash fandom has been tied to the sexual identities of the fans themselves and their queer reading practices. The editors of a special issue of *Transformative Works and Cultures* on "Queer Female Fandom," Eve Ng and Julie L. Russo (2017) observed that femslash characters' sexual and gender identities are often reflected in those of their fans, creating fan communities of predominately queer women. They argued that this correlation makes femslash fandoms powerful platforms to "manifest forms of political agency," enabling them to resist and counter heteronormativities more effectively than other fan groups (Ng & Russo, 2017, para. 2.1). This is certainly evident in studies of the *Xena: Warrior Princess* (Raimi et al., 1995–2001) fandom and their investment in the subtextual queerness of Xena and Gabrielle (Hanmer, 2014; Jones, 2000; Maris, 2016). The emergence of the internet offered fans greater proximity to the show's creators, allowing fans to communicate their desires and expectations directly to producers. Maris (2016) called these incursions technological "queer hacks"—with obvious connotations of subversion and infiltration—and allowed fans to significantly influence creative decisions. More recent scholarship has also explored queer female fans' social media activism as they agitated for improved LGBTQ+ representation onscreen in the wake of Lexa's death (Navar-Gill & Stanfill, 2018; Waggoner, 2018). Femslash fans have been also positioned as critical consumers, labelling Lexa's death as yet another instance of queerbaiting[1] and highlighting the producers' exploitation and manipulation of their queer fanbase (Bridges, 2018; Ng, 2017).

These studies framed femslash fans as resistant, technologically savvy, and innovative participants within convergence culture. However, rather than positioning femslash fandom as wholly subversive, recent work has highlighted how dominant Whiteness continues to structure queer female fan spaces, actively contributing to and reinforcing the marginalisation of femslash fans of colour (De Kosnik & Carrington, 2019; Kumar, 2021; Stanfill, 2019b). Pande and Moitra (2020) explain that queer fans of colour are expected to participate in campaigns promoting queer representation, putting aside their concerns around racism, which are often dismissed or seen as attempts to derail the queer cause. While queer fan activism demands inclusion and diversity onscreen, their campaigns are marked by a "problematic whiteness that forgets and excludes the experiences of queer fans of colour" (Navar-Gill & Stanfill, 2018, p. 98). The field of fan studies has also been criticised for failing to consider the intersectionality of fan experience beyond sexuality and gender (Pande, 2020a). Race is not engaged with in the same depth as issues of gender and sexuality, or it is only discussed in fandoms with a visible "Other" (read: non-White). This neglect minimises and excludes the impact of

---

[1] "Queerbaiting" is a term traditionally used to describe how studios deliberately insert queer subtext in media to deliberately "bait" and exploit viewer investment without intending to actualise queerness onscreen.

race in queer fan experience and further reinforces the default Whiteness of fandom.

The Whiteness of queer media also serves to marginalise femslash fans of colour. In an analysis of queer historical period dramas, Emily Coccia (2022) argues that the historical focus on White histories is reproduced in fans' contemporary investments and fan works. She writes that media and fan investment in wealthy, White historical narratives and characters reproduces structural Whiteness, writing that "in stitching together past and present, this fan recovery project nonetheless reproduces existing hierarchies insofar as it makes wealthy, white histories legible, leaving others unclaimed and unrecognized" (p. 3.5). Even those fan spaces deemed safe for marginalised communities of queer people can reproduce structures of White supremacy, leading to situations where "fan repurposing is subversive in one context (interrupting heteronormative canons) but coercive in another (reinforcing racial power structures)" (Pande, 2018, p. 59). In this contested forum, we see the intersectional identities of fans dictating the degrees to which they are embraced by the mainstream. While the White, middle-class, heterosexual male geek[2] has enjoyed an increased positive reception in mainstream media, this acceptance merely "redefines but does not erase boundaries of exclusion" (Busse, 2015, p. 111)—the mainstream celebration of the fan does not extend to non-White, non-male and non-straight fans and their practices, which continue to be derided.

If the ideal fan is straight, White, and male, then the queer female fan of colour is not imagined as a fan at all. Their fan experiences are the focus of this book. These queer fans face placating propaganda on multiple fronts: that equality has been achieved for LGBTQ+ communities, and that all fans have been embraced by mainstream culture and enjoy a position of cultural power. But as these fans attest in this book, the journey to progress is not linear but haphazard, and liberation for some means the continuation of oppression for others. The fans' experiences reveal that they continue to navigate between assimilation and alienation, and subversion and complicity on multiple identity axes. As Jonathan Gray

---

[2] Once a derogatory euphemism for "fan," the term "geek" has since been reclaimed. Anne Gilbert (2017) notes that the normalisation of fan/geek culture—their expertise in their chosen objects, the accumulation of collectibles, etc—has seen the geek evolve into a more socially acceptable, mainstream figure, leading Aprill Brandon to declare, "it's chic to be geek" (Brandon, 2007).

(2007) argues, "to study fans is to study many of the key structuring mechanisms by which contemporary culture and society work" (p. 16). To this end, a study of *queer female and genderqueer fans* uncovers the messy and fluctuating mechanisms shaping contemporary media engagement and the racialised, heteronormative politics that continue to shape their experiences as queer viewers.

## FINDING TIME IN FEMSLASH FANDOM

This book contributes to the growing body of scholarship on femslash fans but also connects this under-researched area with another—the intersection of queer theory and fan studies. Through the lens of queer temporality, I investigate how queer female and genderqueer fans experience time differently. Several studies have explored this topic, but do not explicitly name them as experiences of queer time. For example, Sara Gwenllian Jones (2000) discusses how the intertextuality of *Xena: Warrior Princess*—where it references historical periods and figures such as Shakespeare, Boudicca, the Amazons, ancient Greek myths and present-day Los Angeles—encourages movement and "propels fans toward other texts, knowledges, and interests" (p. 410). Through this intertextuality, fans are encouraged to move between different histories, reflecting what Annamarie Jagose describes as the "back-to-the-future loops" of queer time (2009, p. 158). More recently, Ellie Turner-Kilburn (2022) and Emily Coccia (2022) analyse queer historical period dramas and frame the fans' practices as attempts to connect with queer female histories and bring them into the present. These studies identify the porous temporal boundaries of femslash fan practices but do not consider them within the context of queer time. This book brings queer temporality into dialogue with fan scholarship to encourage further questions of progress, history, and liberation in contemporary queer viewing experiences.

Eve Ng's (2017) article of queer contextuality has been integral in shaping this approach. Looking at the TV series, *Rizzoli & Isles* and *The 100*, Ng explores how fans discern whether something qualifies as queerbaiting. She argues for a model of "queer contextuality" (para. 2.7) where fans draw on the intertextuality of the text, producer paratexts (such as interviews and social media posts by directors or actors) and previous representations of queer characters in screen media to decide whether a text qualifies as queerbaiting. This model of queer contextuality suggests that fans manoeuvre between past texts and paratextual sources in backwards and lateral movements.

The application of Ng's queer contextuality matrix can be seen in Julie Russo's (2009) investigation of subtextual queerness in the television series, *Law & Order: Special Victims Unit* (Wolf et al., 1999–present). Russo recounts how lesbian fans speculated on the queerness of the character, Detective Olivia Benson, drawing on the masculinisation and connotative queerness of past "working women on screen" such as in *Murphy Brown* (para. 3.3), while also drawing on queer readings of the text itself. To invalidate this fan speculation, the actress portraying Detective Benson gave an interview denying the likelihood of the character being bisexual, with subsequent episodes employing what many fans saw as a "de-dykefication" of the character (para. 5.3). In this matrix, fans drew on past texts, the text itself, and paratextual information to assess the validity of Detective Benson's queerness and the likelihood of the character engaging in a queer relationship in the future. Using Ng's theory of queer contextuality, queer fans negotiated meaning in backwards, lateral, and rhizomatic movements—drawing on the past to evaluate queer representation in the present and to speculate about the future (Aguas, 2019). Through these loops between memories and queer imaginings, the fans move through time, demonstrating how queer temporal flows are integral to queer fan practices.

The temporal movements of the queer contextuality matrix find resonance in the fans' time-travelling wounds after Lexa's death. The queer pain of the past was brought into the present not only through media intertextuality—the repetition of the Bury Your Gays trope—but also through a socio-emotional intertextuality. *Things felt the same as they did before.* While existing studies have explored the fans' past-present intertextualities, this book engages with queer theory to frame these temporal movements as experiences of queer time. If studying fans makes clear the "key structuring mechanisms by which contemporary culture and society work" (Gray, 2007, p. 16), then queer theory's attention to the social construction of normative gender, sexuality, and time makes it an adept partner. This book forges connections between the fields of queer theory and fan studies to offer new and productive perspectives on contemporary queer lives.

Amidst an evolving and dynamic landscape—with the normalisation of (some) fans in convergence culture, an increase in mainstream queer representation, and the growing number of rights afforded to some members of the LGBTQ+ community—the contemporary queer fan negotiates multiple sites of inclusion and alienation. In this period of change and transition, an investigation of queer female and genderqueer fans draws out the temporal discontinuities, displacements, and (backward) detours that mark the contemporary queer fan experience. Using an interdisciplinary approach, this study resists the marginality of queer subjects and challenges the implicit Whiteness of fandom, and fan and queer scholarship.

## REFERENCES

Aguas, E. (2019). The queer temporalities of queerbaiting. In J. Brennan (Ed.), *Queerbaiting and fandom* (pp. 57–59). University of Iowa Press. https://doi. org/10.2307/j.ctvrs8xtj.8

Bacon-Smith, C. (1992). *Enterprising women: Television fandom and the creation of popular myth.* University of Pennsylvania Press.

Brandon, A. (2007, May 4). It's chic to be geek: Comic book fans are proud to be nerds - and everyone else is just trying to catch up. *Tribune Business News,* 1.

Bridges, E. (2018). A genealogy of queerbaiting: Legal codes, production codes, "Bury Your Gays" and "*The 100* Mess". *Journal of Fandom Studies, 6*(2), 115–132. https://doi.org/10.1386/jfs.6.2.115_1

Busse, K. (2015). Fan labor and feminism: Capitalizing on the fannish labor of love. *Cinema Journal, 54*(3), 110–115. https://doi.org/10.1353/cj.2015. 0034

Coccia, E. (2022). Femslash fandom and the cultivation of white queer genealogies: Longing for histories, reading for futures. *Transformative Works and Cultures, 37.* https://doi.org/10.3983/twc.2022.2225

De Kosnik, A., & Carrington, A. (2019). Fans of color, fandoms of color. *Transformative Works and Cultures, 29.* https://doi.org/10.3983/twc.2019.1783

Fiske, J. (1992). The cultural economy of fandom. In L. A. Lewis (Ed.), *The adoring audience* (pp. 38–57). Routledge. https://doi.org/10.4324/978020 3181539-9

Gilbert, A. (2017). Live from Hall H: Fan/Producer symbiosis at San Diego Comic-Con. In J. Gray, C. Sandvoss, & C. Lee Harrington (Eds.), *Fandom: Identities and communities in a mediated world* (2nd ed., pp. 354–368). New York University Press. https://doi.org/10.2307/j.cttlpwtbq2.24

Gray, J. (2007). Introduction: Why study fans. In J. Gray, C. Sandvoss & C. Lee Harrington (Eds.), *Fandom: Identities and communities in a mediated world* (pp. 1–16). New York University Press. https://doi.org/10.2307/j.cttlpw tbq2.3

Gray, J., Sandvoss, C., & Harrington, C. L. (Eds.). (2007). *Fandom: Identities and communities in a mediated world*. New York University Press. https://doi.org/10.2307/j.cttlpwtbq2

Hanmer, R. (2014). Xenasubtexttalk. *Feminist Media Studies, 14*(4), 608–622. https://doi.org/10.1080/14680777.2012.754778

Jagose, A. (2009). Feminism's queer theory. *Feminism & Pyschology, 19*(2), 157–174. https://doi.org/10.1177/0959353509102152

Jenkins, H. (1992). Textual poachers: Television fans and participatory culture. *Routledge*. https://doi.org/10.4324/9780203111339

Jenkins, H. (2006). Convergence culture: Where old and new media collide. *New York University Press*. https://doi.org/10.7551/mitpress/978026203 6016.003.0012

Jones, S. G. (2000). Histories, fictions, and "Xena: Warrior Princess." *Television & New Media, 1*(4), 403–418. https://doi.org/10.1177/152747640 000100403

Kumar, S. (2021). Carmilla fandom as a lesbian community of feeling. *Transformative Works and Cultures, 36*. https://doi.org/10.3983/twc.2021.2007

Maris, E. (2016). Hacking "Xena": Technological innovation and queer influence in the production of mainstream television. *Critical Studies in Media Communication, 33*(1), 123–137. https://doi.org/10.1080/15295036.2015.112 9063

Navar-Gill, A., & Stanfill, M. (2018). "We shouldn't have to trend to make you listen": Queer fan hashtag campaigns as production interventions. *Journal of Film and Video, 70*(3–4), 85–100. https://doi.org/10.5406/jfilmvideo.70. 3-4.0085

Ng, E. (2017). Between text, paratext, and context: Queerbaiting and the contemporary media landscape. *Transformative Works and Cultures, 24*. https://doi.org/10.3983/twc.2017.917

Ng, E., & Russo, J. L. (2017). Envisioning queer female fandom [Editorial]. *Transformative Works and Cultures, 24*. https://doi.org/10.3983/twc.2017. 1168

Pande, R. (2018). *Squee from the margins: Fandom and race*. University of Iowa Press.

Pande, R. (2020a). How (not) to talk about race: A critique of methodological practices in fan studies. *Transformative Works and Cultures, 33*. https://doi. org/10.3983/twc.2020.1737

Pande, R. (Ed.). (2020b). *Fandom, now in color: A collection of voices*. University of Iowa Press.

Pande, R., & Moitra, S. (2020). Whose representation is it anyway? Contemporary debates in femslash fandoms. In R. Pande (Ed.), *Fandom, now in color: A collection of voices* (pp. 151–163). University of Iowa Press.

Raimi, S., Stewart. R. J., & Tapert. R. (Executive Producers). (1995–2001). *Xena: Warrior Princess*. [TV series]. Universal Television.

Russo, J. L. (2009). Sex detectives: *Law & Order: SVU*'s fans, critics, and characters investigate lesbian desire. *Transformative Works and Cultures, 3*. https://doi.org/10.3983/twc.2009.0155

Stanfill, M. (2013). "They're losers, but I know better": Intra-fandom stereotyping and the normalization of the fan subject. *Critical Studies in Media Communication, 30*(2), 117–134. https://doi.org/10.1080/15295036.2012.755053

Stanfill, M. (2018). The unbearable whiteness of fandom and fan studies. In P. Booth (Ed.), *A companion to media fandom and fan studies* (pp. 305–317). Wiley. https://doi.org/10.1002/9781119237211.ch19

Stanfill, M. (2019a). Exploiting fandom: How the media industry seeks to manipulate fans. *University of Iowa Press*. https://doi.org/10.2307/j.ctvd7w89q

Stanfill, M. (2019b). Fans of color in femslash. *Transformative Works and Cultures, 29*. https://doi.org/10.3983/twc.2019.1528

Stitch. (2021a, January 28). Who actually gets to 'escape' into fandom? *Teen Vogue*. https://www.teenvogue.com/story/who-actually-gets-to-escape-into-fandom-column-fan-service

Stitch. (2021b, May 26). 'iCarly' fan misogynoir is part of a larger fandom pattern. *Teen Vogue*. https://www.teenvogue.com/story/icarly-fan-misogynoir-is-part-of-a-larger-fandom-pattern

Turner-Kilburn, E. (2022). Reimagining queer female histories through fandom. *Transformative Works and Cultures, 37*. https://doi.org/10.3983/twc.2022.2109

Waggoner, E. B. (2018). Bury your gays and social media fan response: Television, LGBTQ representation, and communitarian ethics. *Journal of Homosexuality, 65*(13), 1877–1891. https://doi.org/10.1080/00918369.2017.1391015

Wanzo, R. (2015). African American acafandom and other strangers: New genealogies of fan studies. *Transformative Works and Cultures, 20*. https://doi.org/10.3983/twc.2015.0699

Warner, K. J. (2015). ABC's Scandal and Black women's fandom. In E. Levine (Ed.), *Cupcakes, pinterest, and ladyporn: Feminized popular culture in the early twenty-first century* (pp. 32–50). University of Illinois Press.

Wolf, D., Jankowski, P., Forney, A. W., & Martin, J. (Executive Producers). (1999–present). *Law & Order: Special Victims Unit*. [TV series]. Wolf Films; Universal Television.

Zwaan, K., Duits L., & Reijnders, S. (2014). Introduction. In L. Duits, K. Zwaan & S. Reijnders (Eds.), *The Ashgate research companion to fan cultures* (pp. 1–6). Ashgate Publishing. https://doi.org/10.4324/9781315612959-1

# A Queer Ethnography

Does queer theory reside purely in the theoretical? How does queer theory speak to our everyday realities? This research looks at abstract queer theory and the ways it manifests in lived experience. Through ethnographic fieldwork and an affective method of presentation, it explores queer time through participants' written narratives and video testimonials—presenting them in their own voices, in their own bodies, and in their own words.

This ethnographic method differs from common approaches that rely on textual analysis (see Edelman, 2004; Love, 2007; J. E. Muñoz, 2009). For example, in Gary Needham's (2009) study on queer temporalities in the television series, *Torchwood* and *Cold Case*, he draws on textual analyses to illustrate how time-travel narratives, editing, and visual parallels are used to suggest that queer love is "realized through temporal disjuncture... against the normative logic of time's fixity" (p. 154). In his study, textual analysis is the key to unlocking the queer temporalities of the narrative and medium. However, he also states that "the asynchronous and the non-linear are deeply felt" (p. 153). The gap here is the assumption of viewer response rather than engaging with audiences to more effectively illustrate exactly how this is felt and experienced.

This study explores the ongoing tension between abstract theory and the materialities of everyday life. Kath Browne and Catherine Nash (2010) describe how queer theory's reliance on textualism has resulted in a field

29

E. Aguas, *Queer Interruptions*, Palgrave Fan Studies, https://doi.org/10.1007/978-3-031-77025-8_3

"disengaged from understandings of contemporary experiences of sexualities and lived socialities" (p. 13). They point to the need for queer theory to engage with the actual lived experiences of queer people and to involve the communities and materialities of the social worlds under investigation. Echoing this, Alison Rooke (2010) insists on a movement away from "philosophical abstraction and textual criticism," calling for a "queer sociological ethnographic perspective," which grounds theory and engages with the realities of everyday life (p. 26). Rather than "the implied reader and the hypothetical spectator" evident in Needham's imagined audience from earlier, Amy Villarejo (2009) also argues for a methodological shift: with the movement from television to online digital media, there should be a parallel movement away from textual analysis to a consideration of production contexts and an examination of viewer response and practice (p. 50). This research bridges the disciplines of queer theory and fan studies and asks, what do queer temporalities look like in lived experience? How does delay, belatedness, or inertia manifest in everyday life?

Employing a queer of colour methodology further responds to criticism regarding the Whiteness of queer theory and fan studies (Eng et al., 2005; Pande, 2020; Wanzo, 2015). Alongside Suzanna Walter's (1996) assertion that queer theory's implied subject is a universal gay male figure, Lorena Muñoz (2010) argues that the discipline is further "theorised and understood through lenses that are largely academic, western, White, and privileged" (p. 57). L. Muñoz writes that a queer of colour methodology highlights the gendered, classed, and racialised nature of subjects, challenging the implicit Whiteness of queer theory. This research seeks to explore the impact of race in the fans' experiences of heteronormativity and backwardness. It treats Whiteness not as a neutral identity, but as a racialised force that structures time itself. It elevates the voices of queer fans of colour and considers the intersectionality of queer fan experience from multiple positionalities and identities. This research fosters an openness to "multiple ways of seeing" (L. Muñoz, 2010, p. 66), making visible the heterogeneity of my participants and counters the prevailing Whiteness across disciplines.

A queer of colour methodology also emphasises reflexivity and how my multiple subjectivities engage with those of my participants. There is a common misconception that "matching" identities between researchers and their subjects—where they share gender, sexuality, or class identities—produces an "insider" dynamic, resulting in more authoritative and accurate research. However, James McDonald (2013) argues for the multiple identifications of each subject and the "impossibility of simultaneously matching for all categories of difference and individual experiences" (p. 130). Browne and Nash (2010) concede that, as queer thinking argues, subjects and subjectivities are "fluid, unstable and perpetually becoming" (p. 1), calling attention to how multiple subjectivities can align and diverge over the course of the research.

For example, during fieldwork at an LGBTQ+ community centre, Alison Rooke (2010) describes how the performance of her "lesbian cultural capital" (p. 36) made participants more willing to disclose their experiences to her. However, a shift in her sexual identity during the project affected her relationship with participants. Rooke recognised that she and her participants inhabited the category of "lesbian" in different and conflicting ways. The complex and shifting nature of subjectivities is not encompassed by insider/outsider binaries, with Gorman-Murray et al. arguing that "we are all simultaneously insider and outsider" (2010, p. 104).

A "queer reflexivity lens" (McDonald, 2013, p. 128) compels me to recognise the various ways that multiple identities and notions of insider/outsider have impacted on the research process. During participant recruitment, I released a video to online fan networks on Tumblr and X (formerly Twitter) introducing the research and asking fans to participate. The video was designed to be easily shareable and accessible, and I was made visible as a queer fan of colour. I recognised the benefits of performing not only my "lesbian credentials" (Rooke, 2010, p. 36) but also my fan credentials in creating an atmosphere of shared understanding with my participants. This element of insider status reassured fans that the study would reflect the community more sensitively, and that I would be an advocate for queer communities. My Asian identity also suggested that I would investigate issues of race from a position of lived experience. While I successfully "matched" with participants in numerous ways, there was also a need to remain vigilant to my own multiple identifications, and that of my participants. The heterogeneity of femslash fan communities was evidenced by my participants' shifting gender identities throughout the research project, illustrating the fluidity of identification and the fallacy of insider/outsider binaries in research.

A queer ethnography recognises the need to engage with the communities under investigation and considers the intersectionality of the participants' experiences. It counters conceptions of Whiteness as neutral or the default and brings the voices of participants of colour to the fore.

As a reflexive methodology, it emphasises the multiple subjectivities of research participants, and requires an openness to alternative experiences and an acknowledgement of "the messiness of everyday life" (Browne & Nash, 2010, p. 14).

## Recruitment and Interviews

Three groups were targeted for recruitment: (a) self-identifying queer female Clexa fans; (b) academics; and (c) media creators (writers and producers of queer content).

Fan recruitment utilised existing online Clexa fan networks on Tumblr and X. In January 2018, research accounts on Tumblr and X were created, and a short promotional video was released introducing the research project and asking fans to opt-in. Personal contacts within the fan community were also invited to retweet/reblog these requests to reach the broader fanbase. Recruiting participants through primarily anonymous and wide-ranging fan networks on X and Tumblr ensured that the likelihood of preexisting relationships with participants remained low.

After opting in, participants were asked to complete a short email survey. This survey was primarily used to collect information on demographics, sexual orientation, their reactions to Lexa's death, and their experiences of social marginalisation (the different ways they may have felt on the outside" or "out-of-sync" with the world around them).

From this pool of respondents ($n = 72$), seven were invited to participate in in-depth interviews. The interviews were semi-structured, using traditional interview methods of probing and clarifying questions, and were up to 2 hours in duration. The interviews focused on their feelings towards Lexa's death, their experiences of discrimination (sexual, racial, gendered), their experiences as queer fans, and how they engage with media representation. Participants were also asked to expand upon or clarify the answers they had provided in the online surveys. For this reason, the participants' interviews were prioritised over their online survey responses in the book due to their depth and specificity. Conversely, the online survey responses were used in the online documentary website as stand-alone quotes due to their brevity and relevance to the themes explored in each video.

For the in-depth interviews, a range of participants were selected (diverse in age, ethnicity, and geographical location) whose responses could be linked to conceptions of queer time. The screening process prioritised fans travelling to an upcoming ClexaCon[1] fan convention and who were willing to be filmed on-site for the documentary. This selection process was a creative decision that allowed for more significant influence over the aesthetic than interviews with remote fans recorded over Skype. The event took place in Las Vegas in April 2018 and interviews with nine participants were filmed at the convention hotel. It should be acknowledged that these aesthetic requirements also limited the pool of respondents, with most participants residing in North America.

Two academics working or interested in media or fan studies disciplines were identified as potential participants: Dr. Elizabeth Bridges and Dr. Rebecca Hall. They identified as Clexa fans and were attending ClexaCon. Academics were specifically approached to give context to the fans' experiences within media and/or fan studies, presenting scholarship to a lay audience. They were contacted via X and their interviews were filmed during the convention. While Elizabeth and Rebecca were initially approached to provide academic context, their interviews proved to be some of the most emotive, articulate, and compelling responses from fan perspectives. In this study, Elizabeth and Rebecca's identities as Clexa fans have been prioritised over their roles as academics offering scholarly expertise.

Initially, two to three interviews with media creators were planned. However, as a queer fan-centred project, this was reduced to one interview with Javier Grillo-Marxuach (writer and co-executive producer of *The 100*) so as not to privilege an authorial voice over the fans' perspectives and experiences. Grillo-Marxuach was contacted via email (listed on his blog) and his interview was filmed at his home in Los Angeles following ClexaCon. His interview focused on his interactions with fans before and after Lexa's death, how he made sense of the fans' emotional reactions, and reflections on his role in creating content for queer audiences.

Interviews with fans and academics have been used in the book and the online documentary, while the interview with Grillo-Marxuach has been

---

[1] ClexaCon is an LGBTQ+ media convention first held by fans in 2017 to commemorate Clarke and Lexa's relationship. It has since expanded and now attracts up to four thousand fans, academics, actors, and industry personnel each year, creating a community space for surveying and consuming content focused on queer female, trans and non-binary characters.

used in the documentary content to give context to the fans' experiences and present a writer/producer's perspective on Lexa's death.

During data analysis, it became clear that additional interviews were needed to respond to data gathered in the initial round and to present queer theoretical concepts within the documentary. Three additional interviews were scheduled for filming in the United States in January 2019 (to coincide with personal travel), but due to unforeseen circumstances, only one participant could attend their interview. An interview request was sent to an Australian queer theory academic to collect the additional data needed, but the Covid-19 pandemic disrupted the possibilities for interstate travel for filming. Despite these setbacks, I was satisfied that the data collected through the initial interviews and online surveys were sufficient for the book and online documentary. The website design was amended to include additional explanatory text on abstract queer theory and its relevance to my respondents' experiences in the absence of a queer theory academic interviewee.

After the Queer Interruptions website launched in July 2021, several fans and academics shared their reactions to the work with me via private message on X and Tumblr. I chose to expand the limits of the original participant recruitment strategy to include two people who had contacted me about the website and to include our correspondence as data to be analysed. The inclusion criteria remained the same, i.e. self-identifying queer femslash fans but was limited to those with whom I had direct correspondence and who freely shared their reactions to the documentary work. One of these respondents was a Clexa fan who had previously participated in the research through an online survey. Another respondent was a person unknown to me who messaged me via X after seeing the website. Both respondents gave their consent for our personal correspondence to be quoted in the study. As the contours of the research took shape, the need for this data became apparent and I was able to incorporate fan/viewer reception in the critical reflections and analysis of the project's aesthetics and goals.

## STIMULUS MATERIAL

As many participants were unfamiliar with the concept of queer time, I developed stimulus material to assist in exploring this abstract concept. When considering what kinds of stimulus texts would produce the most useful data, I reflected on those texts and passages that had given me

clarity—those "a ha!" moments. Specifically, phrases and synonyms from
the work of Freeman (2010), J. E. Muñoz (2009), and Needham (2009).
From these, I developed a series of six cards with word prompts grouped
thematically (Fig. 3.1). Towards the end of the interview, each word card
was presented to the participant. They were asked whether those phrases
related to their experiences as a queer fan and, if so, in what ways?

**Fig. 3.1** The six stimulus cards used during the in-depth interviews with fans

Drawing on the work of Jukka Törrönen (2002), these stimulus texts were used as "clues" which, together with the interview questions, "conduct[ed] the interviewees to conjectural and metonymic reasoning" (p. 351). The phrases were short and evocative, inviting the participants to consider them in creative ways. The word prompts enabled participants to connect concepts of queer time to their lived experiences using associative links, approaching these theoretical concepts tangentially. By giving them the language and phrases to describe the abstract, the research topic was made "perceptible" and "discernible" for participants, who were then "'empowered' to express their social experience" (pp. 345–346). Rather than prompting further abstract or generalised descriptions, the stimulus cards were able to elicit in-depth descriptions of the participants' experiences (Stacey & Vincent, 2011).

The word prompts encouraged the respondents to narrate their experiences and also introduce unanticipated topics. As Törrönen (2002) writes, "one can use clues to guarantee that the interviewees speak about the basic tensions, ways of action and forms of interaction of the research topic as many-sidedly as possible, without forgetting the relevant contexts" (p. 353). The cards also prompted participants to further elaborate on points they had spoken about earlier in the interview. In this way, the stimulus texts had achieved their intended objective: "*enabling respondents to say more about the subject*" (Chrzanowska, 2002, p. 4, emphasis in original). The use of the six stimulus cards made the research more accessible, concrete, and engaging for participants, producing rich and nuanced data more effectively than traditional interview questioning (Chrzanowska, 2002; Stacey & Vincent, 2011).

However, by screening participants in the recruitment phase and using stimulus materials during the interviews, there was a risk of producing subjective data and privileging the theoretical concepts in the research. Alison Rooke (2010) explains that the relationship between theory and ethnography is a tense one. Citing the work of Willis and Trondman, she states that theory should be employed to provide insight into ethnographic evidence, rather than prioritising theory and then seeking evidence to "prove its validity" (p. 27). In this study, the question is not, do queer people experience queer time? Rather, the focus is on: what does queer time look like in live experienced? What does this tell us about contemporary queerness, the state of progress of LGBTQ+ rights, and how groups continue to be marginalised? The research approached participants with the assumption that they had experienced queer temporalities in some way (validated through the screening process) and employed targeted questions and techniques to solicit relevant data.

Staying faithful to the ethos of queer ethnography, I also needed to remain open to alternative experiences. Not all phrases or stimulus cards resonated with each participant. This was acknowledged at the time and the interview progressed to the next question. Other participants experienced queer temporalities in unexpected ways. For example, one respondent reflected positively on their experience of closeted, adolescent delay as it ensured their safety in a conservative environment. This challenged dominant conceptions of delay as negative and undesirable. This data resonates with Rooke's (2010) assertion that ethnography "offers the possibility of reshaping and fine-tuning theory" through praxis (p. 27).

Conducting the interviews during the ClexaCon event heightened the emotionality of the research. Fans commented on the sense of community, acceptance, and liberation they experienced at the convention, which put into stark relief the discrimination and homophobia they experienced in daily life. However, as discussed in Chapter 2, not all fans experience this sense of community in fandom spaces. For transgender, gender-diverse and queer fans of colour, conventions such as ClexaCon can be spaces of heteronormative subversion while also reinforcing dominant Whiteness (Pande, 2018). For example, due to a lack of queer of colour panels and guests at the first ClexaCon in 2017, my respondent Rebecca Hall, organised an unofficial queer fan of colour panel, which was then incorporated into future iterations of the convention. The ClexaCon fandom space was a complex site of community and alienation; liberation and erasure. That atmosphere shaped the fans' interviews and contributed to the intensely emotional testimonials recorded: haltingly honest, melancholic, and painful memories alongside optimistic and joyful wishes for the future.

This study was performed in line with the principles of the Australian National Statement on Ethical Conduct in Human Research 2007 (Updated 2018).[2] Approval was granted by the Human Research Ethics Committee of the University of Technology Sydney in September 2017 (UTS HREC REF NO. ETH17-1663). Additional ethics clearance was granted in November 2021 (UTS HREC REF NO. ETH21-6591),

---

[2] National Statement on Ethical Conduct in Human Research 2007 (Updated 2018). The National Health and Medical Research Council, the Australian Research Council and Universities Australia. Commonwealth of Australia, Canberra.

approving the use of personal correspondence with respondents. Furthermore, informed consent to participate and publish data was obtained from individual participants.

Each participant was made aware of the probability of being recognised in the documentary by members of their professional or social networks before filming took place. Respondents were given the option to use a pseudonym, both in the book and the documentary footage, though the data has not been de-identified.

## REFERENCES

Aguas, E. (2021, July). *Queer Interruptions.* https://queerinterruptions.com
Browne, K., & Nash, C. J. (Eds.). (2010). *Queer methods and methodologies: Intersecting queer theories and social science research.* Ashgate Publishing. https://doi.org/10.4324/9781315603223-1
Chrzanowska, J. (2002). Interviewing groups and individuals in qualitative market research. *SAGE Publications Ltd.* https://doi.org/10.4135/978184 9209342
Edelman, L. (2004). *No future: Queer theory and the death drive.* Duke University Press.
Eng, D. L., Halberstam, J., & Muñoz, J. E. (2005). Introduction: What's queer about queer studies now? *Social Text, 23*(3–4), 1–17.
Freeman, E. (2010). Time binds: Queer temporalities, queer histories. *Duke University Press.* https://doi.org/10.1215/9780822393184
Gorman-Murray, A., Johnston. L., & Waitt, G. (2010). Queer(ing) communication in research relationships: A conversation about subjectivities, methodologies and ethics. In K. Browne & C. J. Nash (Eds.), *Queer methods and methodologies: Intersecting queer theories and social science research* (pp. 98–112). Ashgate Publishing. https://doi.org/10.4324/9781315603223-7
Love, H. (2007). *Feeling backward: Loss and the politics of queer history.* Harvard University Press.
McDonald, J. (2013). Coming out in the field: A queer reflexive account of shifting researcher identity. *Management Learning, 44*(2), 127–143. https://doi.org/10.1177/1350507612473711
Muñoz, J. E. (2009). *Cruising utopia: The then and there of queer futurity.* New York University Press.
Muñoz, L. (2010). Brown, queer and gendered: Queering the Latina/o 'streetscapes' in Los Angeles. In K. Browne & C. J. Nash (Eds.), *Queer methods and methodologies: Intersecting queer theories and social science research* (pp. 61–72). Ashgate Publishing. https://doi.org/10.4324/9781315603223-4

Needham, G. (2009). Scheduling normativity: Television, the family and queer temporality. In G. Davis & G. Needham (Eds.), *Queer TV: Theories, histories, politics* (pp. 143–158). Routledge.

Pande, R. (2018). *Squee from the margins: Fandom and race*. University of Iowa Press.

Pande, R. (Ed.). (2020). *Fandom, now in color: A collection of voices*. University of Iowa Press.

Rooke, A. (2010). Queer in the field: On emotions, temporality and performativity in ethnography. In K. Browne & C. J. Nash (Eds.), *Queer methods and methodologies: Intersecting queer theories and social science research* (pp. 25–39). Ashgate Publishing. https://doi.org/10.4324/9781315603223-2

Stacey, K., & Vincent, J. (2011). Evaluation of an electronic interview with multimedia stimulus materials for gaining in-depth responses from professionals. *Qualitative Research: QR, 11*(5), 605–624. https://doi.org/10.1177/146 8794111413237

Törrönen, J. (2002). Semiotic theory on qualitative interviewing using stimulus texts. *Qualitative Research, 2*(3), 343–362. https://doi.org/10.1177/146879410200200304

Villarejo, A. (2009). Ethereal queer: Notes on method. In G. Davis & G. Needham (Eds.), *Queer TV: Theories, histories, politics* (pp. 48–62). Routledge.

Walters, S. D. (1996). From here to queer: Radical feminism, postmodernism, and the lesbian menace (or, why can't a woman be more like a fag?). *Signs: Journal of Women in Culture & Society, 21*(4), 830–869. https://doi.org/10.1086/495123

Wanzo, R. (2015). African American acafandom and other strangers: New genealogies of fan studies. *Transformative Works and Cultures, 20*. https://doi.org/10.3983/twc.2015.0699

# CHAPTER 4

# Queer Disorientations: Delay and Extended Adolescence

This chapter extends on Chapter 2 and delves deeper into the ways queer fans continue to be included and/or excluded from the mainstream. It focuses on the fans' experiences of queer temporalities—how they deviate or diverge from heteronormative and racialised timelines—uncovering their experiences of exclusion or empowerment, and everything in between.

Gary Needham (2009) writes that queer people whose lives do not align with heteronormative life narratives centred on marriage and reproduction experience feelings of "asynchrony, discontinuity, belatedness, arrest [and] reversal" (p. 152). Their deviations from the norm are an "embrace [of] temporal displacements" (p. 152)—they are living in queer time. This sense of displacement is seen in the experiences of several of my respondents who expressed feelings of delay when comparing their lives to their heterosexual counterparts, or who described experiencing a prolonged adolescence in their 20s or 30s rather than during their

**Supplementary Information** The online version contains supplementary material available at https://doi.org/10.1007/978-3-031-77025-8_4. The videos can be accessed individually by clicking on the DOI link above or by scanning this link with the SN More Media App.

teenage years. The first section of this chapter delves into these experiences of delay, where the fans' testimonials serve to illustrate what temporal displacement can look like in lived experience.

The second section of this chapter then extends these queer temporalities to the experience of fandom, where dominant stereotypes depict fans as immature and arrested in their development (Jenkins, 1992; Stanfill, 2013). Adult fan engagement is frowned upon as age-inappropriate, where irrational, emotional, and obsessive fan attachments are not the "right way" to interact with media (Harrington & Bielby, 2010). While the White, middle-class, heterosexual male geek has enjoyed growing acceptance in mainstream media, my respondents' continued experiences of racial, gendered, and classed normativities question the extent of mainstream inclusion. As Busse (2015) notes, the celebration of the fan merely "redefines but does not erase boundaries of exclusion" for feminine and queer fans (p. 111).

We can see that the normativities that alienate queer people also work to marginalise fans. For queer fans, the exclusion is two-fold: they are not only alienated due to their queerness, but also due to their subcultural participation. By analysing their experiences through the lens of queer temporalities, we can uncover the prevailing mechanisms that continue to deride queer fans and queer fans of colour. Their testimonials give materiality to queer time: the non-linearity of being caught in varying degrees of acceptance and alienation from the mainstream. And rather than being wholly negative, these messy feelings of displacement or delay prove to be advantageous and liberatory, revealing the alternative and productive pathways of queer fandom.

My online documentary, Queer Interruptions (Aguas, 2021) features two videos aligned with this chapter. The videos can be accessed by clicking on the DOI link provided under the Supplementary Information section of this chapter or by scanning the link with the SN More Media App (Figs. 4.1 and 4.2).

## STRAIGHT TIME AND CHRONONORMATIVITY

In "Happy Futures, Perhaps," Sara Ahmed (2011) suggests that heteronormativities shape our ideas about what constitutes "a good life" and which milestones qualify as "a social good" (p. 164). This ordering of social life is what J. E. Muñoz calls "straight time" (2009, p. 21), where life trajectories often follow the path of birth, adulthood, marriage,

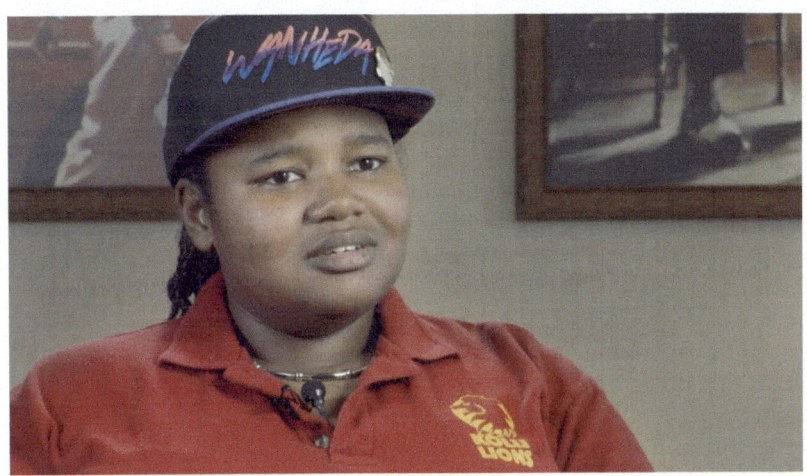

**Fig. 4.1**   A screenshot from *Queer Interruptions: Delay, Belatedness and Wasted Time* (Aguas, 2021)

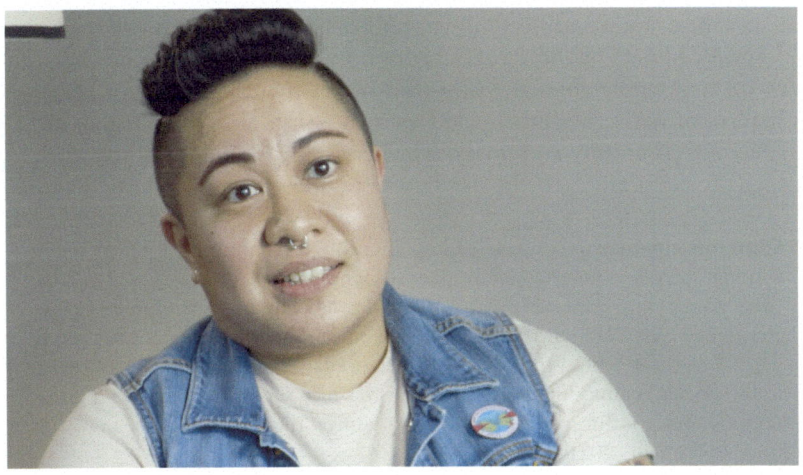

**Fig. 4.2**   A screenshot from *Queer Interruptions: Straight Time and Normativity* (Aguas, 2021)

reproduction, retirement, death, and the passing on of assets to kin. These heteronormative timelines privilege reproduction and shape what constitutes "'successful,' 'important,' and 'significant' relations" (Fenske, 2015, p. 73). However, J. E. Muñoz writes that queer people, in particular those who choose not to be biologically reproductive, are deemed "developmentally stalled" and do not have "the complete life promised by heterosexual temporality" (2009, p. 98). Ahmed states that the queer life is "constructed as an unhappy life... as it lacks certain things: a husband, children" (2011, p. 165). Queer lives often diverge from these life narratives, circumventing and reordering these milestones in backwards and lateral movements. Similarly, Kathryn Bond Stockton (2009) asserts that the term "growing up" connotes a vertical, linear, and forward thrust towards marriage, work, and reproduction in straight time. She argues that queer people diverge from this trajectory, and rather than "growing up," queer people "grow sideways" (p. 6). Against the pervasive linearity of straight time, queer people find themselves out-of-sync—they are growing sideways and feeling backwards.

Elizabeth Freeman (2010) further examines how time is used to regulate, organise, and condition human bodies "toward maximum productivity" (p. 3). She coins the term "chrononormativity" to describe how our lives are temporally aligned with social rituals that privilege reproduction in heteronormative life timelines. Freeman asserts that these rituals act as signifiers of continuity and progress, where these hidden rhythms work to ensure the economic growth of the state. She writes:

> Chrononormativity is a mode of implantation, a technique by which institutional forces come to seem like somatic facts. Schedules, calendars, time zones and even wristwatches inculcate what the sociologist Evitar Zerubavel calls "hidden rhythms," forms of temporal experience that seem natural to those whom they privilege. Manipulations of time convert historically specific regimes of asymmetrical power into seemingly ordinary bodily tempos and routines, which in turn organize the value and meaning of time. (Freeman, 2010, p. 3)

J. Halberstam (2005) also argues that reproduction is tied to rules of respectability and that the scheduling of "repro-time" is seen as "natural and desirable" (p. 5). This scheduling of daily life—"family time"—is also designed to ensure optimal environments for child-rearing (p. 5). While such rituals and institutions are shaped by and uphold heteronormative life tempos, Halberstam asserts that not all gay, lesbian, and transgender people live markedly different lives from their heterosexual peers. With the legalisation of same-sex marriage and the extension of adoption and parenting rights to same-sex couples in countries such as the United States and Australia, lesbians and gay men who subscribe to chrononormative rituals "have entered the repronormative time of parenting" (Freeman, 2010, p. 3).

While some members of the queer community enjoy admittance to straight time institutions and rhythms, it is important to note that several of my respondents have recounted persistent feelings of delay and belatedness and of having to "catch up" to their heterosexual counterparts. For example, respondent Elizabeth Bridges (45 years old, White, she/her, lesbian, Tennessee, U.S., in-person interview[1]) describes feeling "behind" compared to her peers:

> I got married when I was forty-three, and that's a little late. I would say that the timeline for me has not been the standard. I saw straight time happening around me—friends I've gone to high school with etc, who were getting married right out of college, or even maybe right out of high school, depending, and having kids and doing all those things. There were times when I thought, "Ugh, I'm behind." ... A lot of these things were happening for a lot of people around me and I did have this feeling of stasis and "When is my time?" and "Why is this not happening?" and "What's wrong with me?" ... I definitely was aware of that discrepancy while it was happening. I think I've more or less caught up at this point, but it took a little while.

Elizabeth also uses "stagnation" to refer to her adolescent years as she observed her peers "having these 'life experiences' that you're 'supposed' to have," which she was not experiencing. After these feelings of delay and stasis, she explains how markers of adulthood such as buying a home in her 30s and getting married aged 43 contributed to a sense of having "caught up" and adopting a normative timeline, albeit belatedly: "Some of the adult things did come along, maybe at a halfway 'normal' [air quotes gesture] time."

While Elizabeth locates the mid-to-late 1990s as her period of adolescent stasis, these feelings of asynchrony persist for the queer youth

---

[1] All interviews were conducted in accordance with the University of Technology's ethics guidelines, approval number UTS HREC REF NO. ETH17-1663.

of today. For example, respondent Annie Davis (18 years old, White, she/her, queer, Ohio, U.S., online survey) describes her feelings of ostracisation and stasis while attending a private Christian high school:

> I always felt like I was on the outside of things like prom and homecoming, where all my girlfriends would bring their boyfriends as their dates, and I would be sitting dateless in the corner, not telling people that the reason I didn't have a date was because I was queer and afraid to bring a girl. In some ways, I feel like my romantic development was delayed. In middle school, when everyone started dating, I wasn't into the whole dating thing, and now I know why. I didn't really get those "first" experiences most girls do with their boyfriends in middle school, and I, to this day, still haven't experienced my "firsts" with a girl. In some ways, being WLW [a woman-loving-woman] feels like it can set you on the slow track to love and relationships because we have to spend so much time figuring out what we feel and why we feel it. Straight kids can jump into relationships while growing up much easier than gay kids can as it's the "norm" in society to be straight; they don't have to deal with those feelings of confusion that many queer kids do.

For Annie, there is a direct correlation between her queerness and a sense of delay in her romantic development. Several other respondents recounted similar experiences, for example, Kellymarie (30 years old, Mexican American, she/her, lesbian, Wisconsin, U.S., in-person interview):

> I didn't know through high school why I didn't like boys, why I didn't want to date, why it just wasn't interesting to me. I feel like there is a lot of wasted time. I feel like if I was younger and if there was something to show me or guide me to figure out, "Oh hey, this is why you're not following your friends with what they're doing, and there's nothing wrong with that, that's just who you are," it would have saved me a lot of wasted time. I actually bring that up a lot—I was a late starter because of that. I hadn't figured anything out yet. And I was way behind everybody else in experiences and things like that.

For Annie and Kellymarie, the sense of delay was attributed to the time needed to clarify their same-sex desires and the stigma associated with exploring their sexuality within a school context. Corinne Logan and Marla Buchanan (2008) explain in their study on same-sex desire in female adolescents that this sense of delay is a direct result of a homophobic social environment and "a lack of opportunity or a denial of one's same-sex sexual desire" (p. 492). Many of Logan and Buchanan's participants reported having few opportunities to act on their same-sex desires (having their first same-sex encounters at age 18 or older), as well as an absence of queer role models or peers and a lack of social scripts to help them negotiate their same-sex desires. A lack of social scripts resonates with Kellymarie's response where she laments the lack of a "guide," which resulted in her being a "late starter." Their study also highlights the effect of heterosexism and homophobic environments leading to participants' denial and repression of their same-sex desires, as demonstrated in Annie's response where her reluctance to bring a female date to prom stemmed from fear and stigma within her conservative Christian school setting. While Logan and Buchanan do not explicitly reference straight time, the delay that their queer female adolescent participants experience is perceived against the implicitly heteronormative life trajectory of their peers. This research frames these experiences of delay and "wasted time" as temporal displacements within the linearity of straight time and chrononormativity.

Despite the increasing number of rights afforded to gays and lesbians, the pervasive nature of straight time is evidenced by Elizabeth, Annie, and Kellymarie recounting similar experiences of delay despite age gaps that range from 12 to 27 years between them. Their shared experience harks back to Heather Love's notion of mapping continuities between the "bad gay past" (2007, p. 27) and the present, highlighting the similarities between seemingly distant eras. Mapping these continuities between Elizabeth, Annie, and Kellymarie lays bare the immutability of straight time across generations and reveals the "inadequacy of queer narratives of progress" in our liberated present (Love, 2007, p. 27). In exploring these persistent feelings of delay, we can recognise how straight time continues to be enforced, challenging the simplistic chronologies of progress that dominate contemporary LGBTQ+ politics.

A perceived temporal delay in queerness is not new, with early sexological theories positing homosexuals as immature and arrested in their development. Valerie Rohy (2009) writes that these theories drew on the logics of scientific racism: while African Americans were conceived as primitive, backward, and uncivilised, sexologists drew on these evolutionary theories to identify homosexuals as infantile, regressive, and less advanced than their heterosexual counterparts. Rohy's work explores these analogous links, asserting that linear time was used to devalue and marginalise queer and racialised subjects. She argues that straight time is structured by both heterosexuality and Whiteness, where the desirability and linear progress of heterosexuality and Whiteness depends on a queer and non-White opposite. Rohy argues that the "perverse backwardness" of people of colour and queers is used to buttress the linearity of straight, White time, where "the anachronism assigned to blackness and queer-ness is in fact not external, but internal to and constitutive of the white, heterosexual norm" (p. xv). Similarly, Alexander Cho (2015) argues that Western hetero-temporal narratives position the "adult straight white man at the endpoint of psychic maturity" (p. 48), rendering women, queers, and people of colour regressive and deficient.

Rohy's work resonates with Charles W. Mills' (2014) examination of a manufactured and racialised conception of time. Mills argues that, within the colonised regions of Africa and the Americas, time is racialised as White time and shaped by Euro-centric ideas on the appropriate use of time, biological rhythms, work, and leisure. He argues that racial inequalities produce "regimes of temporal exploitation and temporal accumulation" centred on the redistribution of time—taking time away from certain groups and "*transferring* time from one set of lives to another" (p. 28, emphasis in original). Mills writes that this redistribution of time manifests in the Black community's "unequal temporal access to institutions, goods, services, resources, power, and knowledge" (p. 28). Within this temporal regime, unequal access to cultural markers of matu-rity, respectability, and prosperity produces different life rhythms, leading to conceptions of Blackness as unproductive and undeveloped while promoting White heteronormative rhythms as the ideal. Mills writes that Black people in the Americas were considered "premodern, a 'backward' race holding back the nation from moving forward in time," rendering Black time "squandered time, wasted time, a temporality appropriate for a people on whom time itself is wasted" (Mills, 2014, p. 31). Mills' work demonstrates the mechanisms that place Blackness outside of normative White time and echoes Rohy's argument where the apparent anachro-nism of Blackness is not inherent but is manufactured to construct White, heterosexual normativities—White Time.

My investigation into the feelings of delay and stasis recounted by queer fans does not consolidate early sexological theories on homosexual and non-White infantilism but acts as a critique of the fantasy of straight White, normative time. My respondents' delayed development points to the manufactured nature of the heterotemporal ordering of life. Their feelings of delay are not the result of an inherent deficiency in queerness but point to how these anachronistic others are constructed to privilege straight White time and its "natural" rhythms.

The sense of delay or belatedness experienced by my queer respondents of colour should be understood within this complex interplay of racial and heterosexist politics. Rohy (2009) and Mills' (2014) correlation between the implicit Whiteness of straight time and the perceived "backwardness" of African Americans takes on significance for subjects who are both queer and Black. The convergence of heterosexism and racialised time is evident in the experience of my respondent, Jay (22 years old, Black, she/her, bisexual, Maryland, U.S., in-person interview), who was born in Barbados and moved to the United States to attend College. Here, she recounts an instance of homophobic violence and having to navigate the complex intersections of her identity as a Black queer woman:

> The amount of hatred they [Barbadians] have for the LGBT community—it's something you won't hear about because our news doesn't report about it. You only hear about it if you know someone who is gay and who is there. In Jamaica, for example, about two years ago, a friend of mine was stoned. He ran into a store and had to barricade himself until the police came to break out the crowd. And I remember thinking, "Yeah, I can never come out," because I have no idea how my Mum will take it; I have no idea how my Granny will take it. … My mum will constantly be texting me, "Have a boyfriend yet?" And I have to tell her, "No, I'm very much still single." Very much not ready, I think, to start seriously looking for a partner, even though some of my friends or some of my peers have already gotten married or are getting engaged. For me personally, I don't see myself yet at that point where I love myself enough to then be able to love someone else.

Jay elaborates further in a follow-up email:

> I have even heard some hypothesize that pushing the "gay agenda" onto Black people is a way for "whites" to stifle our reproductive rates on a global scale. They see being gay as a sin that initially only white people indulged in because of how deeply in the closet people had to be in order to be safe. Families are not the only ones that disown LGBT+ people—here, whole communities do so under the pretence that they are acting to wipe out our perceived "perversion."

Within the nexus of racialised queerness, Black queer female subjects such as Jay are not only labelled as backwards and less developed under straight White time, but also find themselves out-of-sync with a dominant conception of Blackness. Jay's struggles may be attributed to what Christopher Lewis (2012) argues is a "politics of hegemonic blackness," in which both femininity and homosexuality are perceived as disempowered, vulnerable identities and "ineffectual in the fight against oppression" (p. 158). Within this paradigm, Black queer sexuality is placed in opposition to what is considered "valuable and viable" Black lives (p. 167). Lewis explains that Black women, in particular, are subject to racist charges of sexual perversity under White supremacy. To combat these charges, Black communities are seen to aspire to sexual normativities that "required black women to hide, mute, and/or shield expressions of (queer) sexuality" (p. 160), effectively seeking "the elimination of black lesbianism" (p. 169). A hegemonic Blackness ensured that the "boundaries of blackness … were heavily patrolled not only to keep black queer expressions out" but also to reinforce an "inviolate conception of blackness" (p. 169).

Audre Lorde (1984) also argues that in the fight for racial equality, unity is conflated with homogeneity, leading to the erasure and denial of non-normativities such as Black queer female sexualities. She argues that Black lesbians are considered "a threat to Black nationhood, are consorting with the enemy, are basically un-Black" (p. 121). Beverly Greene (2000) asserts that lesbianism is seen as incompatible with Black identities, leading to accusations of "racial disloyalty" in the fight for acceptance within the dominant culture (Greene, 2000, p. 247). Greene also argues for the importance of positive cultural mirroring in which the affirmation and acceptance displayed by family members and friends allow children to regard themselves positively within their ethnic groups. Greene writes that queer women of colour "seldom receive positive cultural mirroring for the sexual-minority aspect of their identity," which can lead to a delay in integrating their sexual orientation with other aspects of their identity (p. 247).

While a "politics of hegemonic blackness" (Lewis, 2012, p. 158) has been used to combat the racism and sexism of White supremacy, it also serves to marginalise and silence Black queer female sexualities. In their attempts to counter charges of perversity and to garner acceptance within the dominant culture, it is argued that Black communities aspire to adhere to sexual normativities which, as Rohy argues, are heteronormative and implicitly White. Jay's need to hide expressions of her queerness is not only a response to homophobia but also demonstrates an attempt to comply with the politics of hegemonic Blackness, specifically to combat accusations of (Black and queer) sexual depravity and to counter charges of being inauthentically Black. Her sense of belatedness—a delay in coming out, lack of romantic relationships, and an ongoing struggle with internalised homophobia—is not simply attributed to a homophobic environment but should be framed within a complex interchange of racialised heteronormative politics that both respond to, and are constitutive of, one another.

Expanding on Mills' (2014) work on the transference of time between racial groups, Brittney Cooper explores the redistribution of time in her TED talk, *The Racial Politics of Time* (2016). She states that under White time, "we Black people have always been out of time; time does not belong to us" (10:54). She goes on to cite African American author Ta-Nehisi Coates on this "inescapable robbery of time" (9:29):

> We experience time discrimination, he tells us, not just as structural, but as personal: in lost moments of joy, lost moments of connection, lost quality of time with loved ones and lost years of healthy quality of life. (9:46)

Alongside unequal temporal access to institutions and resources, this time *discrimination* is not merely political but uniquely personal and affecting: a robbery of personal joy and happiness. For my respondent, Jay, this loss of time occurs at the juncture of her Black and queer identities:

> There's a part of me—when I was in College, when I had finally said for the first time that I was bisexual—that stopped because I was still trying to get over that word and applying it to myself. I stopped; I checked out for a bit, honestly. I got very depressed. … My teachers were concerned because I was a good student, and suddenly there were weeks at a time where I would just skip random classes; I just couldn't make myself go. I feel like a lot of time was wasted in the respect that, if we weren't so rigid with our beliefs and the way that we just didn't accept anything that seemed wrong, or as they would say "perverse," I feel like if we grew up in a more openly loving—not even just society, maybe just my family—I wouldn't have had to spend so much time, and still spend time, just to accept who I am and love who I am more. I feel I had ended up wasting a lot of time, especially when my grades started dropping. That was just time I can't get back.

This loss of time that Jay "can't get back" is a personal loss: a lack of self-acceptance, a loss of "openly loving" relationships, and a decline in her mental well-being and scholastic achievements. Her feelings of stasis and discontinuity where part of herself "stopped," and the sense of time wasted due to internalised homophobia and a fear of being labelled "perverse" are cruel thefts of time. Jay's emotive response corporealises the experience of asynchrony within straight time and hegemonic Blackness, where these abstractions can have tangible impacts on the simple act of self-love.

The robbery of time also results in a deviation from the chrononormativities of academic and career development for people of colour. Freeman (2010) asserts that chrononormativity extends beyond reproductive and sexual normativities to shape life timings geared "toward maximum productivity": education, work, and wealth accumulation (p. 3). For Jay, this theft of time resulted in a lack of progress and a decline in her academic endeavours. She alludes to a lack of movement and a failure to follow a normative, linear student timeline—"I just couldn't make myself go [to class]." This scholastic deviation from the expected trajectory is paralleled by her experience entering the workforce as an IT intern. She recounts the discrimination she faced as a woman in the field—where male employees "would ask the females to go get coffee"—and her outsider status as a woman of colour who was also queer:

> I don't want to say "hate" but there's a lot of non-acceptance towards letting women into the space or into the field. That only gets worse if you're not a white woman, surprisingly, because there are a lot of men of colour in the field. And then, if they find out you're gay, it just gets even worse. ... It was just not a good experience. And when you combine that with the fact that I'm bi, I was looking for a place that would be more open, and that place was not it. They were the ones who offered me the job, so at that point, I said no, I'm going to have to find something else to do before I can start making a better salary. That place, for a straight person, would have probably been a dream job, honestly. They're a big company; I would have made a lot of money. But just from interning that one year, I could tell it would have been an awful thing to have to go to every day.

As a queer woman of colour, Jay made a deliberate decision to turn away from the expected path towards career development and "a better salary."

Rather than prioritising the avenue that would result in maximum productivity, Jay prioritised her safety and mental well-being. Her choice results in not merely a career delay, but a detour from forward progress and the expected life timings towards growth and prosperity under straight, White time—a "violation of chronology" (Rohy, 2009, p. 127). Freeman (2010) explains that within a chrononormative society geared towards national economic interests, this "sequence of socioeconomically 'productive' moments is what it means to have a life at all" (p. 5). Through her deviation, Jay becomes an improperly temporalised Black body, disconnected from "narratives of movement and change" and unproductive in the eyes of the state (Freeman, 2010, p. 4).

A sense of stasis is also evident in Jay's delay in coming out to her Mother and Grandmother. She explains that career stability and financial independence are essential factors informing her decision, stating, "I know I can't tell them until at least I'm in a place that's more secure." Rather than simply impacting her career trajectory, her deviation from the expected progression has also resulted in a further delay in Jay coming out to her family. The robbery of time suffered by people of colour has robbed Jay of the joys of academic and career success, and the fulfilment and comfort derived from "openly loving" relationships. Jay is robbed of time in both her private and professional spheres and is designated as out-of-sync with the markers of a successful life—a stasis that renders her deviant, unproductive, and devalued.

The theft of time resulting in a lack of productivity is also reflected in the experience of my respondent, Rebecca Hall (55 years old, African American, she/her, lesbian, Utah, U.S., in-person interview). She describes how, while teaching law as a visiting Professor at university, her existence as the single person of colour in the room was seemingly too "confrontational." She was advised to record each calendar date that race was discussed and to "try to do it as little as possible." She explains that the "hypervigilance" needed as a queer woman of colour is a drain on time and resources and has contributed to the lack of progress she has made regarding her academic and professional goals:

> I feel like I could have done so much and given so much back if I wasn't constantly in a state of exhaustion and hypervigilance. On the other hand, I feel like what shapes me and enables me to give what I do give and create what I do create comes from being in that position.

While several participants reflect negatively on this sense of delay and robbery of time, Rebecca credits this time loss and her positionality as a Black, Jewish queer woman for motivating her activist and artistic endeavours. The "exhaustion and hypervigilance" she has experienced has fuelled her activism, productivity, and success, enabling the recent publication of her successful graphic novel, *Wake: The Hidden History of Women-Led Slave Revolts* (2021).

Several other participants also describe belatedness as a necessary part of their development. Participant Nicole Cristina Espinosa (36 years old, Filipinx-American, they/them, queer/fluid/homoflexible, Nevada, U.S., in-person interview) recounts this beneficial delay:

> When I was in high school, I developed a crush on someone I met through Church. And when I realised that it was a crush, I was like, "Oh, ok. So I guess I'm bi, but I'm not going to do anything about it." I think that it was ok that I didn't explore my queerness as a teenager because I think it would have been more dangerous because this was the late 90s. So as much as there is still—or that there definitely is—resistance towards queer folks today for sure, I think that it was different back then and that it was just not a safe time for me to come out. So I think that, yes, I knew I was not straight, but I wasn't going to do anything about it, for survival.
>
> I think that I'm lucky in the sense that, exploring my sexuality in my early 20s and my queerness at the same time, I think that was fine. That was perfect because I was older and not in high school, and my parents didn't have that much control over me because I can't even imagine what would have happened if I came out as a teenager. I wonder if they would have sent me to a rehab camp? I don't know that financially, they could have? But I wonder because there's a lot of money in the Church. I wonder if—and my parents are well-liked—that folks would have pooled money to bring their poor daughter Nicole to a conversion camp. So I'm ok with my trajectory, for sure.

Nicole's decision not to explore their queerness as a teenager parallels Jay's rejection of a lucrative job offer, with each choosing inaction and the "unproductive" path away from progress in a romantic relationship and career advancement, respectively. Freeman asserts that under the temporal regulations of chrononormativity, "having a life entails the ability to narrate it not only in these state-sanctioned terms but also in a novelistic framework: as event-centred, goal-oriented, intentional, and culminating in epiphanies or major transformations" (2010, p. 5).

Having deviated from these productive moments, there is a sense of uncertainty for both Jay and Nicole; their sense of inaction and delay places them in opposition to the goal-oriented thrust of intentional time. If a meaningful life is an intentional life, then the queer life is indeed "constructed as an unhappy life" (Ahmed, 2011, p. 165). Against the intentionality dictated by chrononormativity, queer time can be seen as *un*intentional—interrupted, lateral, rhizomatic, and meandering.

Although dormancy and deferral are perceived as unproductive within chrononormativity, Nicole's deliberate inaction was positive and beneficial, ensuring their safety against the possible threat of forced conversion therapy. Simon Biggs and Svein Olav Daatland (2006) write that while the success of a lifecourse is measured by continuity and progress, there is also a need to recognise the "positive value of discontinuity" (p. 5). They argue that such discontinuity offers a critique of established paradigms of successful—"productive"—living and ageing while also creating alternatives to these expected pathways. For Nicole, discontinuity and inertia acted as a critique of the homophobia of the late 1990s, where their stasis was necessary "for survival" and which allowed them to explore their sexuality later with greater freedom from parental control. Nicole reflects positively on this discontinuity and illustrates what Gary Needham (2009) argues is the refusal of normative time and the acceptance of alternative temporal experiences of delay, belatedness, and time-wasting. The "embrace [of] temporal displacements" (p. 152) is a refusal of the chrononormative and an acceptance of the arrhythmia of queer time.

As demonstrated by my respondents' testimonies and their context in existing literature, an exploration into feelings of delay, belatedness, and lost time highlights the persistence of straight time and chrononormative logics and calls attention to the experience of a queer racialised time. It also leads us to explore how these queer respondents' experiences of asynchrony can be paralleled with their experiences within fandom, where queer subcultural participation blurs the boundaries between adolescence and adulthood.

## Fandom, Extended Adolescence, and Queer Adulthoods

A conflation of subculture with youth culture positions adult fan participation as age-inappropriate and portrays fans as delayed or arrested in their development. However, an investigation into queer female and genderqueer fans' experiences of delay highlights the fluid boundaries between adolescence and adulthood and recognises the potential for alternative queer adulthoods.

Kristen Schilt and Danielle Giffort (2012) argue that subcultural participation is often delineated as the arena of youth, confined to the transitional period of adolescence before being abandoned upon entry into the adult world of employment and reproduction. Sarah Thornton (1995) also writes that youth subcultural participation is seen as an attempt to resist "social ageing" and the financial and emotional commitments of adulthood (p. 60). This conflation of subculture with youth culture is evident in fandom, which has long been equated with adolescence and youthful explorations of identity (Harrington & Bielby, 2010). In *Textual Poachers* (1992), Henry Jenkins explores popular stereotypes about fans in which they are seen as "infantile, emotionally and intellectually immature" and "should move out of their parents' basement" (p. 10). Mel Stanfill (2013) also details the denigration of male fans of *Xena: Warrior Princess* (Raimi et al., 1995–2001), where journalist Neil Lyndon characterises the fans' behaviour as a symptom of "male sexual avoidance, a sitting out of the dance, a diversion from the frightening, high-speed mainline rails of sexual growth into a siding where a breather can be taken" (p. 118). These common stereotypes construct the figure of the fan as delayed and juvenile, and as Rebecca Williams (2011) writes, these stereotypes are also highly gendered. Commonly, "fanboys" are portrayed as nerdy, social misfits preoccupied with learning useless knowledge and collecting merchandise, whereas "fangirls" are seen as immature, "hysterical, excessively emotional, and obsessive" (p. 169). In her examination of the *Doctor Who* (Moffat et al., 2005–present) fandom, Williams explains that (heterosexual) fangirls are mocked and dismissed for their emotional and libidinal attractions to male celebrities. While Williams attributes this denigration to a failure to conform to masculinised fandom practices, I argue that normative temporalities have contributed to the dismissal of female fans—often older or middle-aged—as "giggling schoolgirls" (p. 174). This infantilisation derides female fans for deviating from appropriate adult behaviours and portrays them as immature, regressive, and fixed in a stagnant adolescence.

However, evolving contemporary perceptions of youth and adolescence are challenging negative equations of youth with fandom. Andy Bennett and Paul Hodkinson (2012) argue that the concept of youth has become more fluid with a recognition of the "increasing diversity, complexity and longevity of youth," where the progression to marriage, reproduction, and career advancement are increasingly extended transitions. They write that this prolonged youthfulness exposes the "porous nature of the boundaries between adolescence and adulthood" (p. 1). Halberstam (2005) also argues that queer peoples' prolonged subcultural participation and their refusal to subscribe to heteronormative timelines redefines the "binary of adolescence and adulthood" (p. 161). For queer fans, particularly those who choose not to have children, subcultural participation contributes to their perceived delay and belatedness while also exposing the heterotemporalities that figure them as such. Rather than consolidating negative stereotypes of fans as delayed and immature, an exploration of the prolonged adolescence of queer fans exposes the constructed nature of seemingly natural chrononormativities.

Halberstam (2005) argues that the period of time queer people devote to subcultural participation extends far beyond that of their heterosexual counterparts where, rather than being theorised as a life stage confined to adolescence, queer subcultural involvement can be a lifelong commitment. Halberstam writes that for queer people, "the separation between youth and adulthood simply does not hold, and queer adolescence can extend far beyond one's twenties" (p. 174). For queer participants, their prolonged adolescence places them outside of the heteronormative pathways to adulthood, as evidenced in part by my respondents' previous testimonials.

Jodie Taylor (2010) explains that conceptions of an extended or prolonged adolescence act as a powerful critique of dominant heterotemporalities. In her study on queer middle-aged participants in queer music scenes, Taylor describes how her respondents' participation in dance parties, casual sex, recreational drug use, and unconventional/ non-monogamous relationships deviate from accepted age-appropriate behaviours and "disrupt the heteronormative conventions of ageing" (p. 898). She argues that their subcultural participation should not be seen as "extended, false, destructive or inappropriate 'youthfulness'" but as ways to problematise conceptions of maturity and adulthood (p. 899). This is reflected in the experience of respondent, Rebecca Hall (55), who explains how maturity and adulthood are tied to heteronormative lifecourses and milestones that queer people often diverge from:

A lot of the life-defining markers and signs of maturity are not ours. They're very normatively straight ... but that also creates a lot of possibilities in terms of age being something that much less defines our community.

She explains that deviations from normatively straight timelines blur the boundaries between life stages, rendering age a flexible construct and echoing Halberstam's assertion that such boundaries do not hold for queer people. Alongside Rebecca, several other participants discuss the intergenerational relationships fostered through fandom, indicating the blurred temporalities in their fandom experiences. My pool of participants ranges in age from 18 to 70 years old for a television show marketed towards the young adult demographic. Both the fan space for *The 100* and fandom, in general, are figured as youth spaces in which older fans such as Rebecca may be dismissed as "reluctant exiles" who have failed to relinquish their youthful interests and "become proper adults" (Vroomen, 2004, p. 143). For Rebecca, this deviation from (hetero)normative adulthood "creates a lot of possibilities" and fosters a way of being not bound by rigid timelines and milestones.

The sense of freedom and possibility achieved through nonconformist, extended adulthood is also illustrated in this response from Nicole Cristina Espinosa (36):

I think that being openly queer amongst my family and just living a queer life has really given me a sense of liberation. Whereas my straight friends have a responsibility to adhere to straight time, I don't have to do that. ... If the public belief is that being an adult is to have a house and to have kids and to do all of this under a certain age—I don't adhere to those restrictions. It's so hurtful also to put that much pressure on folks because it doesn't really allow an individual to explore their life. And I wonder if that's where late-in-life queers come from because of this expectation to do A, B and C before you're 30.

At 36 years of age, many aspects of Nicole's life do not conform to dominant ideas around adulthood—they are in a non-monogamous marriage; they do not own a house or have children; they are a mature-aged student currently completing an undergraduate degree, and they are heavily involved in fandom both online and through attendance at conventions ("it has taken over my life"). Compared to their heterosexual peers, they feel "behind" but are content with their trajectory,

"I am 'delayed,' but I feel like it's fine that I'm delayed. I'm ok with being the older cohort among my classmates." Nicole's lifecourse may be part of what Halberstam considers a politics of refusal—"the refusal to grow up and enter the heteronormative adulthoods implied by these concepts of progress and maturity" (2005, p. 179). Halberstam argues that queer subcultural participation challenges these normative conceptions of maturity and allows us to "map out different forms of adulthood" or to refuse it all together and subscribe to "new modes of deliberate deviance" (p. 174). This deviance offers Nicole a sense of liberation, untethered from straight time, and demonstrates a refusal to subscribe to heteronormative temporal institutions to instead embrace new life rhythms.

At the time of the interview, Nicole was coming to terms with their non-binary identity. They described a reluctance to come out as non-binary and non-monogamous to their family, knowing that their parents' acceptance hinged on a perceived commitment to normative timelines:

> I don't know if, like, my fluidity and my queerness is just something that they're going to be like, "Ok yeah, Nicole's queer, that's it." I haven't come out to them as non-binary because I don't think they're gonna get it. And I definitely have not come out to them as non-monogamous. ... But I think now that I'm a little older and I look like I "have my life together" [air quotes], that to see me with another queer person who also seemingly "has their life together," I think they're gonna be comfortable with that—as comfortable as they could be.

For Nicole's parents, their queerness, non-binary gender, and non-monogamy are made more acceptable (read: palatable) if Nicole is perceived to adhere to a chrononormative schedule. To have their "life together" is to be oriented towards "maximum productivity": relationship stability, employment, and wealth accumulation (Freeman, 2010, p. 3). As Marco Wan (2021) writes, transgender, non-binary, and genderqueer identities are made legible and protected under the law through compliance with normative temporalities. He argues that genderqueer identities are made more socially acceptable when framed as unidirectional, forward, and goal-oriented movements to a complete and final "end" identity, from which maturity, adulthood, and (re)productivity are expected to follow. By framing legitimate identity shifts as linear movements from "an

old gender to a new gender, or from a past identity to a future identity," those who inhabit liminality and gender ambiguity are rendered
inauthentic and unintelligible (p. 568). While Nicole's fluid and non-
normative identities place them within a liminal space, for their parents,
seeing Nicole "with another queer person who also seemingly 'has their
life together'" gives the impression of temporal adherence and makes their
relationship legible, valuable, and permissible.

Through prolonged participation, queer fandom offers and actualises
alternative queer lifecourses. This is demonstrated in Elizabeth's (45)
experience where her involvement in fandom offered new possibilities for
her future. She explains that during childhood, other girls would imagine
their "beautiful wedding and princess dress," a fantasy which did not
resonate with her at all: "When I pictured my adult life, I pictured myself
alone because I couldn't imagine marrying a guy, and I didn't know there
was another option." She describes the pervasive heteronormativity of her
childhood as "monotonous" and repetitive: "it seemed like this endless
stretch of 'I guess this is what my life is going to be like.'" Here, she
recounts the first time she attended a convention at 14 years old:

> One of the greatest and one of the best formative experiences I had as
> a young person was going to this Star Trek convention and seeing weird
> adults in full Klingon gear. Them being grown-ups in their 30s, 40s, 50s
> and being in love with Star Trek and being all about Commander Data or
> Counselor Troi—that was the first moment I had where I thought, "Oh,
> there might be a place for me in this world." And where I didn't think,
> "The future is just going to be this, over and over and over again."

This fandom experience interrupted the monotonous rhythms of
heteronormativity that Elizabeth had dreaded by allowing for new visions
of adulthood not tied to conservative notions of maturity which, in her
sphere, were inherently bound to compulsory heterosexuality, marriage,
reproduction, and the family. The *Star Trek* fans' enduring love for the
show and their participation in performative fandom well into their adult
years represented an extension of youthful interests—an extended adolescence. Halberstam (2005) argues that this "stretched-out adolescence"
allows us to redefine the "conventional binary formulation of a life narrative divided by a clear break between youth and adulthood" (p. 153).
While this may also resonate with heterosexual fans, this extension has
particular valence for my queer fan respondents, who are figured as

delayed, belated, and out-of-sync due to their non-normative sexualities. The extended adolescence of nonreproductive queer subcultural participants—such as Elizabeth and Nicole Cristina Espinosa—allows them to formulate new pathways to adulthood that do not follow the heteronormative imperatives of straight time. My participants are living what Jodie Taylor (2010) terms a "queer adulthood": "a way of living one's life that cannot be sequentially mapped onto pre-existing hetero-temporal schemas" (p. 899). Through their extended involvement in queer subculture, these fans' experiences highlight the chrononormativities that frame them as immature and stagnant adolescent fans refusing adult responsibilities, paralleling the larger charges of delay and unproductivity they face as queer people who deviate from straight White time.

## LIVING IN QUEER TIME

What does it mean to live in queer time? What does the theft of time look like? This chapter has offered visions of how queer temporalities may materialise in everyday lives. My respondents' experiences of belatedness—Elizabeth's ruminations on "'When is my time?' and 'Why is this not happening?' and 'What's wrong with me?'"—and the cruel theft of time from Jay and Rebecca point to the ongoing temporal normativities that continue to ostracise queerness. Different life rhythms and timelines, the choice between safety or productivity, and the restriction and inaccessibility of resources all warp time into a non-linear, interrupted, and disjointed experience. My respondents' testimonials reveal the racialised nature of time and heteronormativity and the multiple ways queer people of colour continue to be oppressed despite contemporary narratives of progress. Their experiences of temporal displacement offer a critique of the fantasy of straight, White time and highlight the chrononormativities that continue to place them divergent to desired and socially valued life trajectories.

However, within the context of fandom, these deviations have proven to be productive and liberatory. How queer fans continue to challenge, disrupt, interrupt, and flout persistent heterotemporalities allows us to generate new visions of maturity and adulthood not tied to the linearity of straight time but as legitimate queer adulthoods. The delayed and meandering adulthoods of queer fans resonate with Kathryn Bond Stockton's assertion that queer people do not "grow up" but "grow sideways" (2009, p. 6). Through their prolonged participation in queer fandom, the fans enact a refusal of normative time and its constraints, embodying the transgressive and resilient qualities of queer time.

## REFERENCES

Aguas, E. (2021, July). *Queer Interruptions*. https://queerinterruptions.com

Ahmed, S. (2011). Happy futures, perhaps. In E. McCallum & M. Tuhkanen (Eds.), *Queer times, queer becomings* (pp. 159–182). State University of New York Press.

Bennett, A., & Hodkinson, P. (Eds.). (2012). *Ageing and youth cultures: Music, style and identity*. Berg.

Biggs, S., & Daatland, S. O. (2006). Ageing and diversity: A critical introduction. In S. O. Daatland & S. Biggs (Eds.), *Ageing and diversity: Multiple pathways and cultural migrations* (pp. 1–12). The Policy Press. https://doi.org/10.51952/9781447366560

Brandon, A. (2007, May 4). It's chic to be geek: Comic book fans are proud to be nerds—And everyone else is just trying to catch up. *Tribune Business News*, 1.

Busse, K. (2015). Fan labor and feminism: Capitalizing on the fannish labor of love. *Cinema Journal, 54*(3), 110–115. https://doi.org/10.1353/cj.2015.0034

Cho, A. (2015). Queer reverb: Tumblr, affect, time. In K. Hillis, S. Paasonen & M. Petit (Eds.), *Networked affect* (pp. 43–57). The MIT Press. https://doi.org/10.7551/mitpress/9715.001.0001

Cooper, B. (2016, October). *The racial politics of time* [Video]. TED Conferences. https://www.ted.com/talks/brittney_cooper_the_racial_politics_of_time/transcript

Fenske, M. (2015). Queer assemblages: How to queer a wedding? In D. B Goltz & J. Zingsheim (Eds.), *Queer praxis: Questions for LGBTQ worldmaking* (pp. 55–66). Peter Lang Publishing. https://doi.org/10.3726/978-1-4539-1439-7/16

Freeman, E. (2010). Time binds: Queer temporalities, queer histories. *Duke University Press*. https://doi.org/10.1215/9780822393184

Gilbert, A. (2017). Live from Hall H: Fan/Producer symbiosis at San Diego Comic-Con. In J. Gray, C. Sandvoss & C. Lee Harrington (Eds.), *Fandom: Identities and communities in a mediated world* (2nd ed., pp. 354–368). New York University Press. https://doi.org/10.2307/j.ctt1pwtbq2.24

Greene, B. (2000). African American lesbian and bisexual women. *Journal of Social Issues, 56*(2), 239–249. https://doi.org/10.1111/0022-4537.00163

Hall, R. (2021). *Wake: The hidden history of women-led slave revolts*. Simon & Schuster.

Halberstam, J. (2005). In a queer time and place: Transgender bodies, subcultural lives. *New York University Press.* https://doi.org/10.1007/s10508-007-9224-x

Harrington, C. L., & Bielby, D. (2010). A life course perspective on fandom. *International Journal of Cultural Studies, 13*(5), 429–450. https://doi.org/10.1177/1367877910372702

Jenkins, H. (1992). Textual poachers: Television fans and participatory culture. *Routledge.* https://doi.org/10.4324/9780203114339

Lewis, C. S. (2012). Cultivating black lesbian shamelessness: Alice Walker's "The Color Purple." *Rocky Mountain Review, 66*(2), 158–175. https://doi.org/10.1353/rmr.2012.0027

Logan, C., & Buchanan, M. (2008). Young women's narratives of same-sex sexual desire in adolescence. *Journal of Lesbian Studies, 12*(4), 473–500. https://doi.org/10.1080/10894160802278655

Lorde, A. (1984). *Sister outsider.* Crossing Press.

Love, H. (2007). *Feeling backward: Loss and the politics of queer history.* Harvard University Press.

McDonald, J. (2013). Coming out in the field: A queer reflexive account of shifting researcher identity. *Management Learning, 44*(2), 127–143. https://doi.org/10.1177/1350507612473711

Mills, C. W. (2014). White time: The chronic injustice of ideal theory. *Du Bois Review, 11*(1), 27–42. https://doi.org/10.1017/s1742058x14000022

Moffat, S., Davies, R. T., & Collinson, P. (Executive Producers). (2005–present). *Doctor Who.* [TV series]. BBC Wales; Bad Wolf; British Broadcasting Corporation (BBC).

Muñoz, J. E. (2009). *Cruising utopia: The then and there of queer futurity.* New York University Press.

Needham, G. (2009). Scheduling normativity: Television, the family and queer temporality. In G. Davis & G. Needham (Eds.), *Queer TV: Theories, histories, politics* (pp. 143–158). Routledge.

Raimi, S., Stewart, R. J., & Tapert, R. (Executive Producers). (1995–2001). *Xena: Warrior Princess.* [TV series]. Universal Television.

Rohy, V. (2009). *Anachronism and its others: Sexuality, race, temporality.* State University of New York Press.

Schilt, K., & Giffort, D. (2012). "Strong riot women" and the continuity of feminist subcultural participation. In A. Bennett & P. Hodkinson (Eds.), *Ageing and youth cultures: Music, style and identity* (pp. 146–158). Berg. https://doi.org/10.4324/9781003084426-16

Stanfill, M. (2013). "They're losers, but I know better": Intra-fandom stereotyping and the normalization of the fan subject. *Critical Studies in Media Communication, 30*(2), 117–134. https://doi.org/10.1080/15295036.2012.755053

Stockton, K. B. (2009). The queer child: Or growing sideways in the twentieth century. *Duke University Press*. https://doi.org/10.1215/9780822390268

Taylor, J. (2010). Queer temporalities and the significance of "music scene" participation in the social identities of middle-aged queers. *Sociology, 44*(5), 893–907. https://doi.org/10.1177/0038038510375735

Thornton, S. (1995). *Club cultures—Music, media, and subcultural capital.* Polity Press.

Vroomen, L. (2004). Kate bush: Teen pop and older female fans. In A. Bennett & R. A. Peterson (Eds.), *Music scenes: Local, translocal, and virtual* (pp. 238–252). Vanderbilt University Press. https://doi.org/10.2307/j.ctv17vf74v.19

Wan, M. (2021). Queer temporalities and transgender rights: A Hong Kong case study. *Social & Legal Studies, 30*(4), 563–580. https://doi.org/10.1177/0964663920948950

Williams, R. (2011). Desiring the doctor: Identity, gender and genre in online fandom. In T. Hochscherf & J. Leggott (Eds.), *British science fiction film and television: Critical essays* (pp. 167–177). McFarland. https://doi.org/10.3366/jbctv.2012.0086

# CHAPTER 5

# Queer Death Onscreen: Anachronism, Bad Feelings, and Melancholia

What strikes me most is how many people are (rightly) comparing Lexa's death to Tara's, even though I know they're too young for *Buffy* ... there are so few resonant lesbian storylines that my 37-year-old experience is the same as an 18-year-old's experience because they've gone back and watched everything that mattered. Our collective queer viewing experience, our entire pop culture canon, is the same across decades and generations. That's why Lexa hurts almost every queer woman the same way, no matter how old they are. (Hogan, 2016)

In a series of posts on X, fan and media critic, Heather Hogan (2016) highlights the extent to which queer female death onscreen is a shared experience within femslash fandom. In 2002, fourteen years before Lexa's demise, yet another queer woman, Tara in *Buffy the Vampire Slayer* (Rubel Kuzui et al., 1997–2003), was killed off in similar circumstances to Lexa: both were struck by stray bullets meant for other characters,

---

**Supplementary Information** The online version contains supplementary material available at https://doi.org/10.1007/978-3-031-77025-8_5. The videos can be accessed individually by clicking on the DOI link above or by scanning this link with the SN More Media App.

65

and both had recently found happiness with a female character only moments beforehand. Lexa's death harked back not only to Tara's death but to numerous queer female character deaths attributed to the "Bury Your Gays" trope (also known as the "Dead Lesbian Syndrome"). The queer online magazine, *Autostraddle*, has collated this dark screen history which, as of November 2023, stands at 235 lesbian or bisexual characters killed on television (Riese, 2023). The commonalities between these deaths stretching from 1976 illustrate how time and space have been compressed, resulting in a queer television landscape that is "the same across decades and generations" (Hogan, 2016).

The anachronism that marks the queer viewing experience extends beyond the repetition of tropes to encompass the fans' pain and despair upon reliving these queer deaths. For many, Lexa's demise caused them to relive past homophobic experiences, where her onscreen death resonated with their previous experiences of rejection, erasure, and fear of violence. This chapter explores these time-travelling wounds, specifically how Lexa's death could transport fans to painful personal histories. An examination of the fans' backward movements identifies how the past is in constant engagement with the present—interrogating the felt experience of anachronism. I argue that this lingering in the past is not marked by stasis but is instead a productive and dynamic temporal relationship: by exploring the fans' experiences of backwardness, bad feelings, and melancholia, we can identify how the homophobia of the past continues in the present and challenge linear narratives of progress and liberation, particularly for queer people of colour.

To view the related documentary video on your device, please click on the DOI link provided under the Supplementary Information section of this chapter or scan the link with the SN More Media App (Fig. 5.1).

## "Feeling Backward" and Lingering in Bad Feelings

Elizabeth Freeman (2010) asserts that rather than experiencing time "as seamless, unified and forward moving," the queer experience of time is instead marked by "asynchrony" and "anachronism" (p. xxii). Not only do queer people find themselves out-of-sync with heteronormative life trajectories, but this asynchrony also blurs the boundaries between past, present, and future. In this temporal multiplicity, queer people experience a "stubborn lingering of pastness" (p. 8) and a disruption of the present

**Fig. 5.1**  A screenshot from *Queer Anachronism: Bury Your Gays and "Feeling Backward"* (Aguas, 2021)

by the past. More than a sense of history being alive, this disruptive past-ness is an affective temporal lingering and serves as a form of political activism in response to systemic inequality. As Tamara De Szegheo Lang (2015) argues, the queer impulse to dwell in neglected histories is "a tool to show the pervasiveness of same-sex sexuality, as a form of mourning and commemoration, as a remedy for mainstream disregard, and as a way of giving LGBTQ people a sense of lineage" (p. 231). Jose Esteban Muñoz (1999) also writes that the everyday battles queer people face are imbued with the suffering of queer history, rendering this backwardness an integral part of queer life. The centrality of this haunting past in the queer experience is further echoed by Heather Love (2007), writing that the ever-present pain of queer history is part of "the corporeal and psychic costs of homophobia" (p. 4). As a response to inequality, this persistent sense of pastness is tied to the unceasing grip of ongoing oppression.

The ever-presentness of these painful histories is referenced by Love (2007) when she characterises the contemporary queer experience as "the odd situation of 'looking forward' while we are 'feeling backward'" (p. 27). By "feeling backward," Love refers to the feelings associated with queer suffering in the past: feelings of shame, self-hatred, despair, depression, and loneliness. For Love, feeling backward is a lingering in the feelings associated with a homophobic "bad gay past" (p. 27) depicted in films such as *Boys Don't Cry* (Peirce, 1999) and *Brokeback Mountain* (Lee, 2005); a lingering in the painful memories of queer history. Through lingering in these past injuries, we can map continuities between the queer past and present, identifying the progress made and the inadequacies that persist in the present.

Disruptive temporal connections with the bad gay past are demonstrated by fan reactions to Lexa's death, where several have described how they were made to relive past experiences with homophobia. In a blog post published by respondent, Elizabeth Bridges (45 years old, White, she/her, lesbian, Tennessee, U.S.), she writes:

> Since Thursday's episode I've been bombarded relentlessly by unbidden memories of every hurt that has ever stung me for being gay, every death or loss I've ever felt in my life. (Bridges, 2016)

She explains that Lexa's death harked back to the harrowing instances of homophobia she experienced while growing up in a fundamentalist Christian environment—from being condemned by her father (a Southern Baptist preacher), to fearing for her safety and having thoughts of suicide. She elaborates further during an in-person interview:

> I felt, personally, like this was a dig. This was a [mimes stabbing motion] into our community. And this is a result of homophobia that's been ingrained for years and years through this use of this trope. And I re-experienced every homophobic thing that I'd ever experienced. I had to re-process all the stuff with my parents, and I actually ended up going to therapy over the summer after that because it was just churning up all this stuff for me from the past that I kind of thought I had dealt with, but I really hadn't. I guess we could call that a blessing? That I got the chance to work through some of this stuff, but it was horrendous, and I don't appreciate it. I don't appreciate being forced into that situation by having to re-experience it through this traumatic moment on a show.

Elizabeth describes Lexa's death via the "Bury Your Gays" trope as a "pure jolt of homophobia" and witnessing this onscreen had a direct and immediate temporal connection to her past experiences of marginalisation. These "unbidden memories" act as connections across temporal landscapes, where the history of queer pain reaches into the present as a disruptive, pervasive, and "stubborn" force (Freeman, 2010, p. 8).

Elizabeth's affective temporal connection to the bad gay past exemplifies Love's (2007) notion of "feeling backward." In her response below, Elizabeth demonstrates how affective continuities between the past and present lead us to question the progress achieved in contemporary LGBTQ+ rights:

> It just reminded me that I'm not normal. I'm not okay in their eyes. I will never be okay. I will always be a lesbian first, and Elizabeth second [crying]. And that was heartbreaking to me. It was not only heartbreaking to me, but it was heartbreaking to me for all these young people who are getting hit with that reality. ... And I thought we were better than that. I thought all of us had come out in the 80s and 90s and early 2000s to make a world where they didn't have to deal with that. And to me, Lexa's death really signified, "Nope. Nope. Not yet."

For Elizabeth, these backward feelings are an experience of anachronism: not only has the past been transposed into the present, but these feelings are anachronistic in the contemporary political context. Elizabeth explains that Lexa's death took place after the legalisation of same-sex marriage in the United States and during an atmosphere of optimism in the fight for equality. While entry into heteronormative institutions has granted rights and protections to some gays and lesbians, other members of the queer community, particularly transgender people and queer people of colour, continue to be excluded. Despite ongoing discrimination, Sarah Schulman (2012) argues that narratives of progress are used as "placating propaganda" to pacify queer communities with the illusion that equality has already been achieved (p. 66). As De Szegheo Lang (2015) asserts, the neo-liberal agenda to portray queer lives as consistently improving serves to construct certain societies or cultures as more progressive than others while working to obscure the continuing marginalisation of queer people. Elizabeth's anachronistic feelings resist placating propaganda by blurring the boundaries between the bad gay past and the present and drawing out their similarities and continuities.

A disruptive pastness and a lingering in queer history challenge the coherence of progress narratives that depend on clear delineations between a homophobic past and a liberated present:

> To validate the present, there must be a past that has been overcome. For the lives of LGBTQ people today to be *better than*, the lives of LGBTQ people in the past have to have been *worse than*. For LGBTQ people today

to be *happy*, LGBTQ people in the past have to have been *hopeless*. (De
Szegheo Lang, 2015, p. 235, emphasis in original)

For Elizabeth, the hopelessness she experienced after Lexa's death
mirrored the hopelessness of decades past—despair she thought had been
overcome. Her feelings of despondency are not relegated to a distant,
unjust history but stubbornly persist in the present. In an age of placating
propaganda, gay pride marches, and a "politics of optimism" (Love, 2007,
p. 29), the persistence of "bad feelings" (p. 161) associated with the past
is an anachronism—the feelings of the bad gay past are anachronistic in
our liberatory present. Love argues that these backward feelings "serve
as an index to the ruined state of the social world" (p. 27), allowing us
to see that the homophobic past is not so far removed from the present.
This queer anachronistic turn backward serves as a mechanism enabling
us to recognise the ongoing violence that punctuates the everyday lives
of queer people and to resist the pacification of oppressed communities.

My participants' emotional interviews illustrate how an anachronistic
lingering in the past is a bodily experience. Elizabeth became visibly
distressed while narrating her experiences. She did not seek to halt the
interview but persevered and openly wept while recounting her feelings
of hopelessness. Her deeply emotional responses point to the viscerality
of temporal displacement. As Freeman (2010) writes:

> For when Prince Hamlet says that "time is out of joint," he describes time
> as if its heterogeneity feels like a skeletal, or at least deeply somatic, dislo-
> cation. In this famous phrase, time has, indeed *is*, a body; the disruption
> of the present by the past and the resulting disunity of the present seem
> visceral. (p. 14, emphasis in original)

For Elizabeth, the "pure jolt of homophobia" cast by Lexa's death
propels her back in time. Her figurative movement is given corporeal
form, capable of being "bombarded relentlessly" and suffering from
time-travelling wounds. Identifying with the queer pain of the homophobic past results in temporal dissonance and a jarring realisation of the
ceaseless disunity of an unequal world. For Elizabeth, this experience of
anachronism elicits profound despair and heartache.

The affective and bodily experience of anachronism is also demonstrated by the experience of respondent Rae D. Magdon (27 years old,
White, she/her, queer/bisexual, Florida, U.S., in-person interview):

I really have to summon my courage and bravery before I watch anything with sapphic women in it or read anything with sapphic women in it. I'm always afraid that one of the lesbian characters will die or get hurt or fall into some other harmful trope, and it hits me deep. It hits me deep. Lexa's death was a very physical sensation: a literal punch to the gut. It hurt so much emotionally that it also hurt physically for a long time. My throat still tightens when I think about it. My anxiety disorder worsened for several months after 307 [season 3, episode 7] aired.

Rae's fears are based on historical precedent: from 1930, the Motion Picture Production Code (also known as the Hays Code) was used to censor and marginalise homosexuality in Hollywood cinema. This code forbid "sex perversion or any inference of it" (Bridges, 2018, p. 125) and eliminated or punished perceived homosexuality, relegating queerness to subtext and giving rise to plot devices such as the "Bury Your Gays" trope. For Rae, Lexa's death was not only the repetition of a deadly trope but also a reliving of the history of queer death and the elimination, punishment, relegation, and marginalisation of queerness onscreen. Her ever-present fear for the fate of lesbian characters reveals the immediacy of the past to the present, and with Lexa's death, an eventual blurring between these boundaries. Rae's experience of anachronism parallels Elizabeth's, where this dislocation is felt on and through the body with both using terms alluding to a physical and violent assault: struck by a jolt and a punch to the gut. My respondents' testimonials reveal how their deviation from the normative flow of time is made tangible and visceral—a lived experience of backwardness felt as distress and bodily injury.

The depth to which this temporal dissonance is a felt experience is evident in Freeman's (2010) work on "chrononormativity," in which time is used to regulate, organise, and condition human bodies towards various heteronormativities (p. 3). Certain experiences come to "feel right" through proper temporal regulation, whereas "the experience of not fitting in often feels both like having the wrong body and like living in a different time zone" (Freeman, 2010, p. 172). This temporal and bodily incongruence is evident in Rae's experience of feeling "out of place":

I feel like I belong to a time ahead of this one, almost. My Grandma—her safe place is the 1950s—she says, "I wish things were still like the 1950s" because she's a cisgender, White lady who had a good marriage. I keep thinking, can we just jump fifty years in the future when maybe things might be better? I just feel out of place in this time. I feel like the world is slowing to a crawl and doesn't want to catch up with where, morally, I feel it should be. I definitely feel a sense of displacement, for sure. It's like, "Are we still having these same arguments about whether we're people? Can we please move on?"

Rae identifies those who fall outside White heteronormativity as exiled from the present and from the past. Deviating from normativity and dominant social scripts, queer people follow alternative temporal rhythms: they often feel out-of-sync and out-of-place.

Sara Ahmed (2004) also references this exile and unbelonging, explaining that "normativity is comfortable for those who can inhabit it" (p. 147). Ahmed argues that the discomfort queer people feel when faced with the heteronormativity of the world around them is "disorienting: one's body feels out of place, awkward, unsettled" (p. 148). Rae's sense of stasis in the advancement of LGBTQ+ rights results in a feeling of disorientation: she belongs to a queer future but exists in a backward present. Her experience of anachronism echoes that of Elizabeth, whose realisation of the nearness of the bad gay past to the liberated present was "like the rug getting ripped out from under you." This queer discomfort and distress make us highly attuned to bodily experience, an "acute awareness of the surface of one's body, which appears *as* surface, when one cannot inhabit the social skin, which is shaped by some bodies, and not others" (Ahmed, 2004, p. 148, emphasis in original). The temporal disorientation Rae and Elizabeth feel is corporeal, and its bodily surfaces sustain these anachronistic jolts and punches—the time-travelling wounds of enduring homophobia.

For Rae, Lexa's death triggered a jarring resurgence of bad feelings and illustrates how the queer pain of the past disorients the present. She explains:

Lexa's death brought up so many painful memories. It was devastating. My parents are homophobic—they're the nicest homophobes you'll ever meet. But they're very religious, they're Greek Orthodox, and they believe that same-gender relationships are wrong. I went to conversion therapy, actually. And one of the things that the priest at conversion therapy said to me was, "You know that you can't be happy in a lesbian relationship. You know they don't end well. You know they're not healthy, right?" And that idea was literally articulated to me from a religious figure when I was only sixteen. And to see it play out onscreen, to see the truth of that statement before my very eyes in a show that I thought was safe, to see a character that I related to so much die in such a convoluted and ridiculous way—it was heartbreaking. It brought me back to that time when I was told that I couldn't be happy.

Rae's response reflects her multitemporality: not only does she experience a movement backward to linger in the pain of the past, but queer unhappiness itself is temporalised as deviant. Ahmed (2011) writes that heteronormativity shapes our ideas about what qualifies as worthwhile and valuable life paths. These lifecourse trajectories privilege marriage and reproduction, where adherence to these timelines promise happiness. In this way, heteronormative culture generates "happiness scripts," which serve as "straightening devices" used to enforce heterosexuality and align the population with the accepted trajectory (Ahmed, 2010, p. 91). However, queer lives often diverge from these life narratives, circumventing and reordering these milestones in backward and lateral movements. Due to this temporal divergence, Ahmed writes that the queer life is seen as an "unhappy life," lacking the rituals and milestones that promise happiness (p. 93). As seen in the priest's intimidation of Rae, to deviate from these happiness scripts is to be "threatened with unhappiness" (p. 91). For Rae, Lexa's death was the fulfilment of this threat played out onscreen—"You know they don't end well"—and transported Rae backward to when she was warned she "couldn't be happy." This achronological "touch across time" (Dinshaw, 1999, p. 21) allows Rae to recognise the continued enforcement of heteronormative happiness scripts and shows how the abhorrent homophobia she experienced in the past retained its grip in the present.

Rae's divergence from heteronormative happiness scripts renders her an unhappy figure, incompatible with images of a queer, liberated present. Ahmed (2010) writes that being attuned to the figure of the unhappy queer can be "an enduring sign of how unbearable it can still be to live in this world" (Ahmed, 2010, p. 105). She asserts that a preoccupation with narratives of progress and "happy queers" conceals "the unhappiness of this world" and the "ongoing realities of discrimination, non-recognition, and violence" that queer people face (p. 106). Both Love (2007) and Ahmed argue against the illusion of a disconnect between painful histories and the present and instead seek to reveal the continuities between eras. Dwelling on the devastation and backward feelings Rae experiences reveals the porous boundaries between the past and present, highlighting the enduring figure of the unhappy queer under persistent hegemonic heteronormativity.

## QUEER MELANCHOLIA AS PRODUCTIVE
## REENCOUNTERS WITH THE PAST

The fans' experiences of anachronism, bad feelings, and unhappiness can also be identified as melancholia. While Freud categorised this mental state as a pathology, contemporary critical race, and queer theorists have explored melancholia as a symptom of the systemic oppression suffered by minority groups. In "Mourning and Melancholia," Freud (1917/1957) distinguishes between the two processes of dealing with loss: mourning as a healthy course of grieving that allows the subject to "let go" of the lost object, giving them the freedom to take on new emotional investments; and its obverse melancholia as a pathological fixation with the lost object and an inability to move on, resulting in a sense of stasis. Eng and Kazanjian (2003) assert that these two processes have distinct orientations towards the past: "unlike mourning, in which the past is declared resolved, finished, and dead, in melancholia the past remains steadfastly alive in the present" (p. 4). The past is kept alive through this repetition, and its meanings and significance continually change in a temporally and spatially dynamic relationship (p. 4).

Scholars have applied this paradigm to critical race theory to illuminate the "psychic impact of racism as a form of loss and trauma" (Cvetkovich, 2012, p. 135). Eng and Han (2003) explain in their study on Asian American students that the experience of assimilation is defined by loss: the failure to achieve dominant cultural norms and ideals of "whiteness, heterosexuality, middle-class family values—often foreclosed to them" (p. 344). For people of colour, the White ideal remains an unattainable fantasy, rendering assimilation a "suspended, conflicted, and unresolved" process (Eng & Han, 2003, p. 345). Rather than following a linear path to an end goal, they grapple with unachievable assimilation, oscillating between feelings of attachment and loss for their country of origin and White America, between racial inclusion and exclusion. For people of colour, racial melancholia is an irresolute process of loss and ambivalence, rendered unresolved and unceasing under dominant Whiteness.

Melancholia has been utilised to describe the struggle of all those who fail to attain the ideals under White heteronormativity, including queer people. Ahmed (2004) argues that queer assimilation into heteronormative institutions such as marriage entails similar forms of attachment and estrangement: a desire to aspire to, and feelings of alienation from the ideals that subjugate queer lives as failed. This identification "with that which he cannot be, and indeed with what has already rejected him" (p. 150) results in a melancholic process of loss and ambivalence. Ahmed poses the question, "How does it feel to inhabit a body that fails to reproduce an ideal?" (p. 146). This question resonates with the experiences of my respondents, Elizabeth and Rae, whose failure to adhere to chrononormative happiness scripts results in an experience of queer melancholia.

This study frames the fans' sense of loss as their failure to inhabit normative ideals. For queer fans, Lexa's death was a melancholic reminder of the ongoing status of queer people as failed subjects, unable to attain the ideals of heterosexuality and for whom assimilation—and happiness— remains elusive. How Lexa's death could transport fans backward to painful memories is not merely a fixation on past injury but part of a melancholic response to the process of assimilation. For Elizabeth and Rae, the pain of Lexa's death as a failed subject speaks to the pain suffered under condemnation by authority figures: Elizabeth's father and Rae's priest at conversion therapy. Her death creates a temporal link to previous experiences of discrimination and homophobia—to previous instances where their failure to live up to the ideal was made clear. Lexa's onscreen death was not merely the loss of a beloved fictional character but is tethered to all losses suffered under heteronormativity: my respondents' loss of familial bonds, belonging, safety, comfort, and future happiness.

The way Elizabeth and Rae were forced to relive past trauma and bad feelings resonates with Wen Liu's characterisation of melancholia as "reencounters" and "ongoing reinvestments" with loss (2019, p. 189). Under persistent heteronormativity, their melancholia consists of backward- forward, past-present movements where aspirations for assimilation are interrupted by these reencounters with discrimination and backward feelings. These temporal oscillations speak to Rae's experience of dislocation—"I just feel out of place in this time"—and the nowhere of unresolved assimilation: between inclusion and exclusion, aspiration and alienation, and acceptance and erasure. Not only is the disjuncture of time felt on the body as jolts and punches, but the body itself is made to feel in flux—out-of-place between a traumatic past, an inadequate present, and an "impossible elsewhere" (Love, 2007, p. 131).

The capacity of queer loss to cross temporal boundaries has made queer lives intimately connected to the pain and sorrow of the past. Love (2007) argues that the "historical impossibility of same-sex desire" has marked queerness with an overwhelming sense of "failure, impossibility and loss" (p. 21). This history of abjection pervades the everyday lives of queer people and its injuries are felt in each melancholic reencounter with marginalisation. As J. E. Muñoz (1999) writes, queer melancholia compels us to "take our dead with us to the various battles we must wage in their names—and in our names" (p. 74). The fans' melancholia carries the pain of queer history through time. This temporal tether is not linear but rhizomatic and recurrent, crossing time through reencounters and re-engagements with bad feelings. Love (2007) argues that this intimacy between the suffering of the past and present highlights "the material and structural continuities between these two eras" (p. 21), exposing ongoing systems of oppression and the inadequacies of progress. The hopelessness and despair Elizabeth and Rae continue to feel illustrate this perpetual link to queer loss and how the violence of the past maintains its capacity to wound and injure in the present.

Despite an historical association of queerness with impossibility and loss, a scholarly preoccupation with bad feelings—trauma, melancholy, loss, and failure—risks pathologising queerness and reinforcing early sexological theories which posited homosexuals as perverse and regressive (Love, 2007; Rohy, 2009). Ann Cvetkovich writes in *An Archive of Feelings: Trauma, Sexuality, and Lesbian Public Cultures* (2003) that both trauma and homosexuality were pathologised in order to construct normative identities, labelling others as abnormal or perverse. Her work depathologises trauma and its "archive of feelings"—shame, grief, rage, loss—by divorcing it from medical discourse and exposing its roots in systemic oppression. Rather than indicating individual pathology, J. E. Muñoz (1999) argues that melancholia is an integral part of everyday life for "communities under siege... part of the process of dealing with all the catastrophes that occur in the lives of people of color, lesbians, and gay men" (p. 74). The trauma and melancholy experienced by my respondents—Elizabeth requiring therapy and Rae's anxiety disorder worsening—are not due to personal failings but are instead responses to ongoing social marginalisation. Elizabeth's familial rejection and Rae's harrowing experience at conversion therapy are not merely isolated incidents but part of what Cvetkovich has identified as the "insidious trauma" of heteronormativity (2003, p. 46). The psychic distress suffered under this hegemony is felt in the "textures of everyday experience" (p. 3) and, in the case of my respondents, extends to a seemingly innocuous television death.

The tethering of queerness to a perpetual sense of loss has led some theorists to question the political utility of melancholia and bad feelings in the fight for equality. While Love (2007) argues that these backward feelings allow us to recognise the political work that still needs to be done, Wendy Brown (2003) asserts that the condition is one of stasis and inaction:

> The irony of melancholia, of course, is that attachment to the object of one's sorrowful loss supersedes any desire to recover from this loss, to live free of it in the present, to be unburdened by it. This is what renders melancholia a persistent condition, a state, indeed, a structure of desire, rather than a transient response to death or loss. (Brown, 2003, p. 459)

She argues that, in protesting marginalisation, the political Left becomes "attached to its own exclusion": its very existence is predicated and subsists on enduring subordination (1993, p. 406). Brown asserts that this perpetuation of "wounded attachments" (1993, p. 391) creates a melancholic political collective that is self-indulgent and stubbornly backward, rendering it ineffective and disinterested in real social change:

> A Left that has become more attached to its impossibility than to its potential fruitfulness, a Left that is most at home dwelling not in hopefulness but in its own marginality and failure, a Left that is thus caught in a structure of melancholic attachment to a certain strain of its own dead past, whose spirit is ghostly, whose structure of desire is backward looking and punishing. (Brown, 2003, p. 464)

A fixation on woundedness is reflected in Elizabeth and Rae's experiences of reliving past trauma: an interminable dwelling in "marginality and failure." Returning to linger on the abjection of the past, they consciously turn away from hope, the future, and possibility. Through their inability to overcome previous trauma—rooted in a homophobic, fundamentalist upbringing and undergoing conversion therapy—they are impeding their own happiness and the collective happiness of queer people (Ahmed, 2010).

Love (2007) also examines the pessimism of melancholia and looking backward where, "paralysed by grief" (p. 128), we are overwhelmed with defeat and rendered impotent: "there are ways of feeling bad that do not make us feel like fighting back" (p. 14). This sense of passivity is evident in the response of Rebecca Hall (55 years old, African American, she/her, lesbian, Utah, U.S., in-person interview):

> When Lexa was killed, what was noticeable about my own personal reaction was how different it was from the younger fans. Mine was more resigned. And in retrospect, I feel almost ashamed of myself. … I don't think I had the emotional reaction that a lot of people had, or maybe I was just inured to it? I turned immediately to the fanfiction. I was just like, "fuck this," and started reading fanfiction, which is what we did with *Xena*. They killed her; they decapitated her—I mean, it was horrific. That was devastating to me. I think I just didn't let myself get attached that way again, if that makes any sense? When your expectations are sub-basement, maybe it just is a little different.

For Rebecca, Lexa's death connects to a long history of onscreen marginalisation through the death of the (subtextually queer) lead character in *Xena: Warrior Princess* (Raimi et al., 1995–2001). This traumatic history of queer female character death leaves Rebecca with a sense of hopelessness and resignation: she has been inured not only to the use of the trope but also to queer abjection and erasure. Her "sub-basement" expectations and refusal to become emotionally invested in queer characters can be seen as a turning away from hope and potentiality—an act of submission in persistent melancholia. Love (2007) argues that, while bad feelings allow us to identify continuities between the queer suffering of the past and that of the present, it does not always follow that we can "turn grief into grievance—to address the larger social structures, the regimes of domination, that are at the root of such pain" (Love, 2007, p. 151). Although Love cautions against the potential for debilitating apathy, she also argues that it is necessary, and indeed possible, to turn backward and engage with negative affect to instigate social change. The tension between activism and acquiescence—between "productive" and "paralysing" melancholia (Love, 2007, p. 150)—resonates with the melancholic oscillations between alienation and identification. While Rebecca's initial reaction to Lexa's death was one of "shameful" inaction and hopelessness, her turn towards fanfiction[1] can be considered an effective form of queer world-building.

J. E. Muñoz (1999) also writes that the backwardness of melancholia is not detrimental but is a generative "structure of feeling" and an integral part of daily life for queer people and people of colour (p. 74). He argues that these ever-present legacies of loss do not inhibit activism but serve as an impetus for communities to mobilise against oppression. In contrast to Brown's (2003) conception as a self-indulgent and self-sabotaging condition, J. E. Muñoz considers melancholia and its backward turn a necessary and effective mechanism to combat inequality and remake the world. The productive potential of this pessimism is evident in how Rebecca's sub-basement expectations served as the impetus for her to embark on a "Het Strike"—where she refused to watch "any media that has straight people in it"—and surprisingly discovered a wealth of queer content and queer creators to support. Rather than being counterproductive and passive, Rebecca's turn away from hope is a bold act of defiance: an adamant dissatisfaction with, and refusal to accept continuing inequalities.

The political utility of melancholia and bad feelings is also evident in the activism of many Clexa fans in the aftermath of Lexa's death. Elizabeth's backward feelings were the catalyst for her to publish her experiences in her personal blog article, "Someday. Maybe. But Not Today" (2016), which drew attention to the continuing use of the "Bury Your Gays" trope and has since been quoted in mainstream news sources such as *Variety* (Ryan, 2016). Her academic activism also exhibits a melancholic turn backward, linking the historical criminalisation and baiting of homosexuals to the mechanics of contemporary onscreen queerbaiting (Bridges, 2018). Rae's sense of hopelessness motivated her and others to purchase over 500 e-books of queer fiction to donate to devastated fans, "so over 500 people got to read a happy, lesbian story after 307 [season 3, episode 7] aired."

Fans also channelled their grief into activism, coming together to hold the first ClexaCon in 2017, a queer media convention that attracts up to four thousand fans, academics, actors, and industry personnel each year, creating a community space for surveying and consuming queer content.

---

[1] Rather than meaning-making remaining in the hands of showrunners and creators, fanfiction allows fans to create their own narratives using existing fictional characters and worlds. As a productive engagement with the source text, fanfiction often seeks to critique, elaborate upon or repair aspects of the original material.

They also began raising funds for The Trevor Project, a charity that assists LGBTQ+ youth in crisis and as of November 2023, they have raised over USD 178,000. The fundraising page became a site of collective grieving as donors published online dedications[2] describing their despair and past and present struggles with homophobia. The website's collection of fan dedications constitutes an "archive of feelings" (Cvetkovich, 2003, p. 7) and demonstrates the devastation of melancholia and its capacity to fuel meaningful social action. Rather than paralysing fans with grief, melancholia allowed them to identify persistent injustices and the fallacies of narratives of progress, where feeling backward is necessary to mobilise the "political energy of unhappy queers" (Ahmed, 2010, p. 106).

The productive potential of melancholia is also evident in its capacity to expose colonial legacies in the present. As a Black, Jewish queer woman, Rebecca's complex positionality pits her against not only the insidious trauma of heteronormativity but also that of White supremacy—"I'm fighting twenty other battles." Her experience of a queer, racialised melancholia uncovers the continuation of anti-Black violence and marginalisation in White supremacist social institutions, media representation, and queer fan spaces. While there has been an increasing number of rights afforded to some members of the LGBTQ+ community (namely White, economically mobile gays and lesbians), the persistence of Rebecca's bad feelings points to the continuing denigration of queer people of colour, particularly within an emerging White homonormativity (Halberstam, 2005; J. E. Muñoz, 1999). Rather than promising a future "hospitable to all," Carillo Rowe et al. argue that the progress made in contemporary gay and lesbian politics merely promises that "it gets better for some" (2015, p. 36).

For Rebecca, an engagement with painful histories and negative affect—trauma, melancholia, anger, and hopelessness—constitutes an integral part of her activism. She explains:

> Our existence and what we're going through today is fully informed by our past. So if our memory is not longer than our lifetimes, then we're really confused. Because then we have no idea like, why are these police killing us? Why is there all this misogynoir? Why are Black women seen as kind of sub-human? Or incapable of feeling pain or suffering? If we

---

[2] The fans' online dedications can be seen on The Trevor Project "Leskru" fundraising website: https://give.thetrevorproject.org/fundraiser/625415 (Tass, 2016).

don't understand the history of slavery, how that institution developed and how it was regulated and maintained, we just have no context for understanding really basic things about our life experience today and how we could possibly move forward to a better future.

Liu (2019) argues that rather than demonstrating an inability to overcome the past, a queer, racialised melancholia is a process of *"dwelling"* that enables us to feel uniquely attuned "to the history and presence of colonial relations" (p. 189, emphasis in original). Rebecca's continuous engagement with the past challenges the illusion of a violent colonial history severed from the present and allows her to identify the enduring historical inequalities that continue to shape the contemporary Black queer experience.

To view the related documentary video on your device, please click on the DOI link provided under the Supplementary Information section of this chapter or scan the link with the SN More Media App (Fig. 5.2).

Éva Tettenborn (2006) also argues for the "transgressive, powerful and political potential" (p. 118) of melancholia when living in the afterlives of slavery. She writes that an active engagement with the past recuperates histories that were lost, suppressed, or erased:

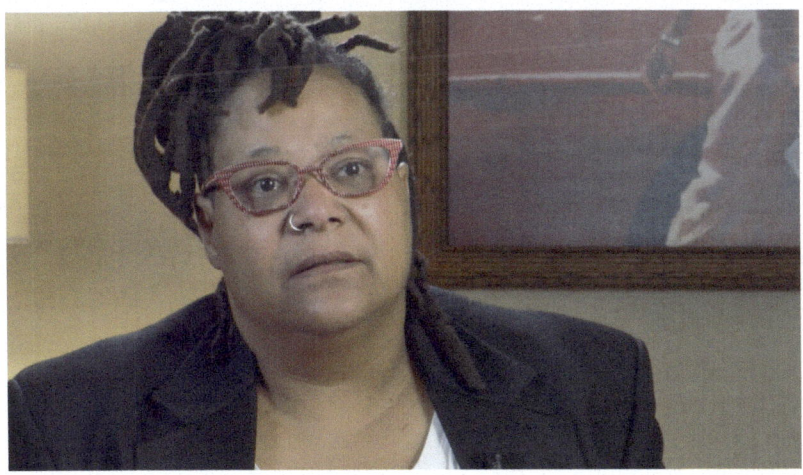

**Fig. 5.2** A screenshot from *"This time doesn't have a place for me"—With Dr Rebecca Hall* (Aguas, 2021)

African American melancholia does not recognize only the survivor's productive aggression against the hegemonic historiography; it also empowers all of those lost objects—African Americans whose life stories were somehow "lost" in white historiography or ignored by a hegemonic perspective on the past. These lost objects are empowered by making an active aesthetic effort to remember, rewrite, or imagine the stories of those lost who demand a proper place in historiography and memory. (p. 115)

For Tettenborn, African American melancholia is a mechanism to resist the Whitening and erasure of Black history. This dwelling in the past is a way to reclaim disavowed lost objects: not only lost histories but a reclamation of the right to mourn Black losses. She explains that enslaved people were made to mask their melancholy—being made to dance and sing at auction and barred from mourning the death of their loved ones— in order to deny the existence of Black subjectivity and render them merely as non-responsive, unfeeling objects. Feeling loss, sadness, and melancholy was a privilege for White enslavers, whose emotional needs superseded those of enslaved people. In response to these ungrieved losses, Rebecca's dwelling is a way to bring the lost mourning of the past into the present and restoring its "proper place in historiography and memory" (Tettenborn, 2006, p. 115).

Melancholia's temporal transference of grief is also explored in the work of Jermaine Singleton (2015), who argues that due to continuing racial oppression, contemporary African Americans have been made to "inherit the unclaimed psychical baggage of their forbears" (p. 52). He explains that while the racial oppression of their enslaved ancestors differs from the oppression faced today, the Black experience is still marked by traces of its legacy: a "transgenerational haunting" that "connects them emotionally to their social history of bondage and exploitation" (p. 54). Through these affective connections, they are "psychologically imprisoned by the same hegemony that held their ancestors in bondage" (p. 57). Singleton asserts that these "unresolved racial grievances" (p. 58) bind racialised subjects across time and space, past and present.

When Rebecca asserts that an understanding of the history of slavery is needed to understand the present experience, she speaks of a transgenerational haunting that carries the emotional and psychic wounds suffered by her ancestors into the present. This haunting is not only an intimacy between past and present inequalities but an emotional intimacy with those whose losses were repudiated and unacknowledged. Rebecca's insistent need to turn backward is a reclamation of unmourned racial losses: of Black lives, history, and subjectivity. Her melancholia is not a "disabling condition" but a powerful "political act" (Tettenborn, 2006, p. 117) and an integral part of reclaiming Black history.

The political utility of Rebecca's anachronistic turn is evident in her activism to recentre enslaved women in historical accounts of resistance, recently publishing a successful graphic novel, *Wake: The Hidden History of Women-Led Slave Revolts* (2021). Her melancholia allows her to recover unresolved and unspoken losses, not to declare them dead and bygone, but to acknowledge their persistence in her current struggles with White supremacist patriarchy and foster an emotional intimacy with her forebears. As a fan, the need to recover Black and queer losses also motivated Rebecca to form a "protest panel" at the first ClexaCon in 2017. Responding to a distinct lack of queer people of colour both as panellists and areas of discussion, Rebecca organised a guerilla "Queer Women of Colour Representation in the Media" panel. Rebecca's activism highlighted the inherent Whiteness of queer fan spaces and the media, exemplifying how these fan spaces can be both subversive (queer) and normative (White) (Pande, 2018). Her protest panel and feelings of exclusion run counter to Hogan's claim on X at the beginning of this chapter that "Lexa hurts almost every queer woman the same way, no matter how old they are" (Hogan, 2016). This statement collapses difference and ignores the impact of race in queer fandom. For Rebecca, Lexa's death spoke to the disavowal of queerness and highlighted the colonial legacies that continue to shape media and fandom. Her activism was motivated by a desire to recover queer Black subjectivities from not only heteronormativity but also White supremacy. For Rebecca, a melancholic process of dwelling and turning backward engenders agency and is an integral tool of resistance and empowerment, a political act against historical and continuing hegemonic White heteronormativity in fan spaces and beyond.

Rebecca's experience as a Black lesbian in a White queer fandom is an experience of racialised melancholia with constant oscillations between inclusion and exclusion. The queer Clexa fan space is overwhelmingly White: Clarke and Lexa are read as a White same-sex couple, and the majority of the show's cast are White. As Rebecca Wanzo (2015) writes, Black fans are seen to be "choosing otherness when they are part of fan communities that allegedly do not speak to their cultural backgrounds or contexts" (para. 2.7). However, she argues that this reading ignores the myriad reasons Black fans may participate in predominantly White fan spaces. Rather than simply "embracing alterity by choice" (para. 2.1), Black fans may experience both "otherness" and "sameness" (para. 2.7). For example, Rebecca recalled being attracted to television shows that combined science fiction and alternative timelines or universes with queer content such as *Xena: Warrior Princess* (Raimi et al., 1995–2001), *Babylon 5* (Netter & Straczynski, 1993–1998), *Wynonna Earp* (Adams & Dennis, 2016–2021), *Carmilla* (Garvie et al., 2014–2016) and *The 100* (Morgenstein & Rothenberg, 2014–2020), which are all dominated by White characters and fandoms. Her "Het Strike"—where she refused to watch "any media that has straight people in it"—used queerness as the qualifying factor. Her involvement in White queer fandoms may be attributed to a shared queer identity but may also be due to a lack of diverse queer representation. For Rebecca, the White fan space was alienating, but the queerness of the space also offered some measure of acceptance. As Wen Liu (2019) explains, "queers of color are perpetually immersed in a melancholic process," constantly preoccupied with feelings of "ambivalence and estrangement" from a Whitening of both heteronormative and queer ideals. This unattainable Whiteness results in a "perpetual grief for the loss of place" (p. 179), evidenced by Rebecca's participation in ClexaCon and her protest against its program. Her complex positionality means she must choose both "otherness" and "sameness", highlighting her persistent melancholic experiences of alienation and inclusion.

Rebecca's melancholic oscillations between otherness and sameness also extend to her feelings of (un)belonging in the Black community. She explains:

> I was actually at a Black women's healing retreat in November, and I was the only queer woman at the retreat. And I'm hanging out with all these straight, Black women, and you know, what they read, the movies they've seen, it's like everything—their culture, their everything—was just different from mine.
> Audre Lorde famously said that we Black lesbians live in the house of difference. That there isn't really a space that's our space, that we can retreat to and then come back and join the coalition fully.

Rebecca's displacement speaks to the historical disavowal of queer sexualities in Black communities. Christopher Lewis (2012) explains that a "politics of hegemonic blackness" (p. 167) developed to construct a normative Black ideal able to counter White supremacy—an "inviolate conception of blackness" (p. 169). Under this hegemony, both femininity and homosexuality are seen as disempowered, vulnerable identities and are placed in opposition to what is considered "valuable and viable" Black lives (p. 167). Audre Lorde (1984) also argues that Black lesbians are considered "a threat to Black nationhood, are consorting with the enemy, are basically un-Black" (p. 121). Lesbianism is seen as incompatible with Black identities, leading to accusations of "racial disloyalty" in the fight for acceptance within the dominant culture (Greene, 2000, p. 247). In queer, Black, or fan spaces intended to foster a sense of belonging, Rebecca's bad feelings instead emphasise the "similar dynamics of regulation and control" (Liu, 2019, p. 189), which marginalise Black queerness and female subjectivity across communities.

Rebecca's racial melancholia is triggered by a failure to attain not only a White ideal under White supremacy but also a normative Black ideal under a hegemonic conception of Blackness. As an inheritance of "unclaimed psychical baggage" (Singleton, 2015, p. 52) from the past, these melancholic bad feelings bring the unmourned losses of a disavowed Black queerness into the present. Her feelings of alienation among a group of Black women are feelings of being un-Black—that she experiences these feelings of exclusion at a women's "healing retreat" is a cruel irony. She perseveres amid constant tension between her identities: in queer fan spaces, she is *too Black*; at her Black women's retreat, her queerness renders her *not Black enough*. These multiple states of unbelonging result in constant oscillations between "exhaustion and hypervigilance."

While the death of a fictional queer character may seem innocuous, it speaks to a vast history of unmourned losses and their enduring corporeal and psychic wounds. Rebecca's melancholic loss of space renders her an anachronistic figure, tethered to the perpetual pastness of the present and placing her outside of chronology. Her loss of space is also a loss of time, opportunity, and possibility. This is the unhappiness, the bad feelings, and the *not enough* of queer racial melancholia.

However, Ahmed (2010) writes that, for people of colour, consciousness of systemic oppression is interpreted as a melancholic attachment to injury. Through their fixation on racism, they "preserve its power to govern social life by not getting over it" (p. 143). Rather than an indication of ongoing inequality, the alienation they purportedly feel is caused by a preoccupation with their own exclusion:

> If racism is preserved *only* in migrants' memory and consciousness, then racism would "go away" if only they would let it go away, if only they too would declare it gone. (p. 148, emphasis in original)

Similar accusations can be levelled at those who continue to repeat narratives of homophobia. In contrast, Liu (2019) validates these backward feelings by framing these repetitive experiences of estrangement as reencounters with "historical and structural trauma" (p. 188). Rebecca's protest panel and dwelling on racism is not an attachment to obsolete history but a declaration of unhappiness with a persistent colonial legacy. Rather than a stubborn "holding on" to illusory racism and homophobia, Rebecca's struggles with unbelonging are reencounters with the present-pastness of Black and queer loss. Each experience of exclusion is a tether across time, entangling the past with the present in temporal multiplicity. Rebecca's loss of place is not only spatial but also temporal: exclusion and alienation are felt as a temporal dislocation. As a melancholic process, this temporal entanglement is unceasing; Rebecca's consciousness of difference will persist as long as White supremacist heteronormativity continues to structure everyday reality.

## UNHAPPY QUEERS

The fans' melancholic experiences illustrate that queerness is not inherently unhappy, but reencounters with a world that is historically and presently unhappy with queer love can cause unhappiness. Ahmed (2010) argues that these anachronistic bad feelings serve as an indication that "these histories persist, and we must persist in declaring our unhappiness with their persistence" (p. 159). She writes further:

> The unhappy queer is unhappy with the world that reads queers as unhappy. The risk of promoting the happy queer is that the unhappiness of this world could disappear from view. *We must stay unhappy with this world*. (p. 105, emphasis in original)

While Brown (2003) views the melancholic as consciously choosing to remain unhappy, the work of J. E. Muñoz (1999) and Ahmed (2010) make clear that, when faced with the ongoing violence of oppression, queer people have no choice but to feel unhappy. Similarly, Liu (2019) argues that melancholia can be characterised as "a refusal to 'feel better'" (p. 181) when met with continuing injustices under White heteropatriarchy. To turn away from hope and to "choose" unhappiness is a productive engagement with negative affect and an awareness of the enduring inadequacies of this world, motivating us to resist and persist.

As some sectors of the LGBTQ+ community gain increasing access to rights and privileges, the queer impulse to turn backward has been replaced by the impulse to forget. Love (2007) writes:

> Given the new opportunities available to *some* gays and lesbians, the temptation to forget—to forget the outrages and humiliations of gay and lesbian history and to ignore the ongoing suffering of those not borne up by the rising tide of gay normalization—is stronger than ever. (p. 10, emphasis in original)

She argues that in an age of advancement where "gays and lesbians have no excuse for feeling bad" (p. 146), we must continue to turn backward, lingering in the queer losses of the past and remaining vigilant to how these losses bleed into the present. Tamara De Szegheo Lang (2015) also emphasises the importance of crossing temporal boundaries and "remaining open to forgotten memories" (p. 240), arguing that "a desiring turn to the complex past might lead to a more critical interpretation of LGBTQ politics today" (De Szegheo Lang, 2015, p. 241). A conscious turn backward to engage with the nuances of queer history is essential to moving LGBTQ+ politics beyond simplified narratives of an oppressive past severed from a liberated present.

This research constitutes a desiring turn backward to dwell in the pain of queer histories, drawing out the structural and emotional continuities across time and challenging the temporal linearity, dominance, and coherence of progress narratives. An investigation into how Lexa's death could transport queer fans to painful personal histories uncovers the time-travelling wounds that persist despite advancements in LGBTQ+ rights. The fans' backward movements highlight the similarities between the bad gay past and the liberatory present, challenging illusions of a violent, oppressive history that has been overcome. The fans' experiences of back-wardness, bad feelings, and melancholia—of temporal dislocation; of a body in flux; of wounds, jolts, and punches where the history of queer pain reaches into the present—is framed not as a pathology, but as a legit-imate response to ongoing systemic oppression. Contrary to claims that it is "just a TV show," for these queer fans, the death of a fictional queer character serves as a reminder that assimilation for queer people remains elusive, trapping them in the void of an unachievable goal: between inclu-sion and exclusion, aspiration and alienation, acceptance and erasure. For Black and queer fans such as Rebecca Hall, a queer character death onscreen constructs a temporal tether, bringing the unmourned losses of a disavowed Black queerness into the present. Rather than being debil-itating and paralysing, this intimacy between the suffering of the past and the pain of the present can mobilise the radical political potential of queerness, evident in the fans' activism after Lexa's death. Their melan-cholic temporal multiplicity and inhabitance of queer time are deviations from rigid chronology, allowing them the freedom to refuse happiness and hope and to instead dwell in the political potential and necessity of bad feelings.

## REFERENCES

Adams, T., & Dennis, B. (Executive Producers). (2016–2021). *Wynonna Earp* [TV series]. Image Comics; Seven24 Films.

Aguas, E. (2021, July). *Queer Interruptions*. https://queerinterruptions.com

Ahmed, S. (2004). *The cultural politics of emotion*. Routledge.

Ahmed, S. (2010). *The promise of happiness*. Duke University Press.

Ahmed, S. (2011). Happy futures, perhaps. In E. McCallum & M. Tuhkanen (Eds.), *Queer times, queer becomings* (pp. 159–182). State University of New York Press.

Bridges, E. (2016, March 7). *Someday. Maybe. But not today*. The Uncanny Valley. http://uncannyvalley.me/2016/03/the100s3e7/

Bridges, E. (2018). A genealogy of queerbaiting: Legal codes, production codes, "Bury Your Gays" and "*The 100* Mess". *Journal of Fandom Studies, 6*(2), 115–132. https://doi.org/10.1386/jfs.6.2.115_1

Brown, W. (1993). Wounded attachments. *Political Theory, 21*(3), 390–410. https://doi.org/10.1177/0090591793021003003

Brown, W. (2003). Resisting left melancholia. In D. L. Eng & D. Kazanjian (Eds.), *Loss: The politics of mourning* (pp. 458–465). University of California Press. https://doi.org/10.1525/9780520936270-022

Carrillo Rowe, A., Tiffe, R., Goltz, D. B., Zingsheim, J., Bagley, M., & Malhotra, S. (2015). Queer love: Queering coalitional politics. In D. B. Goltz & J. Zingsheim (Eds.), *Queer praxis: Questions for LGBTQ worldmaking* (pp. 123–139). Peter Lang Publishing. https://doi.org/10.3726/978-1-4539-1439-7

Cvetkovich, A. (2003). An archive of feelings: Trauma, sexuality, and lesbian public cultures. *Duke University Press*. https://doi.org/10.1215/978082238 4434

Cvetkovich, A. (2012). Depression is ordinary: Public feelings and Saidiya Hartman's "Lose Your Mother." *Feminist Theory, 13*(2), 131–146 https://doi.org/10.1177/1464700112442641

De Szegheo Lang, T. (2015). The demand to progress: Critical nostalgia in LGBTQ cultural memory. *Journal of Lesbian Studies, 19*(2), 230–248. https://doi.org/10.1080/10894160.2015.970976

Dinshaw, C. (1999). *Getting medieval: Sexualities and communities, pre- and postmodern.* Duke University Press. https://doi.org/10.17077/1536-8742. 1471

Eng, D. L., & Han, S. (2003). A dialogue on racial melancholia. In D. L. Eng & D. Kazanjian (Eds.), *Loss: The politics of mourning* (pp. 343–371). University of California Press. https://doi.org/10.1525/9780520936270-018

Eng, D. L., & Kazanjian, D. (Eds.). (2003). *Loss: The politics of mourning.* University of California Press.

Freeman, E. (2010). Time binds: Queer temporalities, queer histories. *Duke University Press.* https://doi.org/10.1215/9780822393184

Freud, S. (1957). *The standard edition of the complete psychological works of Sigmund Freud, volume xiv (1914–1916): On the history of the psycho-analytic movement, papers on metapsychology and other works* (J. Strachey, Trans.). The Hogarth Press. (Original work published 1917). https://doi.org/10.1080/00029157.1996.10403343

Garvie, S., Jennings, C., & Whitney-Vernon, K. (Executive Producers). (2014–2016). *Carmilla* [TV series]. Smokebomb Entertainment; Shaftesbury Films; Shift2; Shift Brand Integration Group.

Greene, B. (2000). African American lesbian and bisexual women. *Journal of Social Issues, 56*(2), 239–249. https://doi.org/10.1111/0022-4537.00163

Halberstam, J. (2005). In a queer time and place: Transgender bodies, subcultural lives. *New York University Press.* https://doi.org/10.1007/s10508-007-9224-x

Hall, R. (2021). *Wake: The hidden history of women-led slave revolts.* Simon & Schuster.

Hogan, H. [@theheatherhogan]. (2016, March 4). *What strikes me most is how many people are (rightly) comparing Lexa's death to Tara's, even though I know they're.* Twitter. https://twitter.com/theheatherhogan/status/705814 487786512384

Lee, A. (Director). (2005). *Brokeback Mountain*. [Film]. Focus Features; River Road Entertainment; Alberta Film Entertainment; Good Machine.

Lewis, C. S. (2012). Cultivating black lesbian shamelessness: Alice Walker's "The Color Purple." *Rocky Mountain Review, 66*(2), 158–175. https://doi.org/10.1353/rmr.2012.0027

Liu, W. (2019). Narrating against assimilation and the empire: Diasporic mourning and queer Asian melancholia. *WSQ: Women's Studies Quarterly, 47*(1), 176–192. https://doi.org/10.1353/wsq.2019.0020

Lorde, A. (1984). *Sister outsider*. Crossing Press.

Love, H. (2007). *Feeling backward: Loss and the politics of queer history*. Harvard University Press.

Morgenstein, L., & Rothenberg, J. (Executive Producers). (2014–2020). *The 100* [TV series]. Alloy Entertainment; CBS Television Studios; Warner Bros. Television.

Muñoz, J. E. (1999). *Disidentifications: Queers of color and the performance of politics*. University of Minnesota Press.

Netter, D., & Straczynski, J. M. (Executive Producers). (1993–1998). *Babylon 5* [TV series]. Warner Home Video; Babylonian Productions; Time Warner; Warner Bros. Entertainment; Warner Bros. Television.

Pande, R. (2018). *Squee from the margins: Fandom and race*. University of Iowa Press.

Peirce, K. (Director). (1999). *Boys Don't Cry*. [Film]. Fox Searchlight Pictures; The Independent Film Channel Productions; Killer Films; Hart Sharp Entertainment.

Raimi, S., Stewart, R. J., & Tapert, R. (Executive Producers). (1995–2001). *Xena: Warrior Princess*. [TV series]. Universal Television.

Riese. (2023, February 27). *All 235 dead lesbian and bisexual characters on TV, and how they died*. Autostraddle. Retrieved November 18, 2023, from https://www.autostraddle.com/all-65-dead-lesbian-and-bisexual-characters-on-tv-and-how-they-died-312315/

Rohy, V. (2009). *Anachronism and its others: Sexuality, race, temporality*. State University of New York Press.

Rubel Kuzui, F., Kuzui, K., Whedon, J., Berman, G., Gallin, S., & Noxon, M. (Executive Producers). (1997–2003). *Buffy the Vampire Slayer*. [TV series]. Mutant Enemy; Kuzui Enterprises; Sandollar Television; 20th Century Fox Television.

Ryan, M. (2016, March 14). "The 100" Lexa mess: What TV, Jason Rothenberg can learn. *Variety*. http://variety.com/2016/tv/opinion/the-100-lexa-jason-rothenberg-1201729110/

Schulman, S. (2012). *The gentrification of the mind: Witness to a lost imagination*. University of California Press.

Singleton, J. (2015). Cultural melancholy: Readings of race, impossible mourning, and African American ritual. *University of Illinois Press*. https:// doi.org/10.5406/illinois/9780252039621.001.0001

Tass, G. (2016). *Leskru*. Fundraising for The Trevor Project. https://give.thetre vorproject.org/fundraiser/625415

Tettenborn, É. (2006). Melancholia as resistance in contemporary African American literature. *MELUS, 31*(3), 101–121. https://doi.org/10.1093/melus/31.3.101

Wanzo, R. (2015). African American acafandom and other strangers: New genealogies of fan studies. *Transformative Works and Cultures, 20*. https:// doi.org/10.3983/twc.2015.0699

# CHAPTER 6

# Queer Interruptions: A Fan Gift and Queer Archive of Feelings

The multimedia component of this study is an online documentary titled, Queer Interruptions (www.queerinterruptions.com). The creative work allows for alternative pathways to investigate how queer fans experience queer temporalities—how they are captured in body language, tone, and what remains unsaid. Utilising documentary video and the affordances of website media, the work offers materials and experiences that the print book cannot. Translating the fans' testimonials to sound and vision allows for affective explorations of the tensions between abstract queer theory and lived experience. As a transmedia work of scholarship, the book and online documentary are complementary, while also provoking critical reflection upon one another (Balsamo, 2011).

As an interactive documentary (i-doc), Queer Interruptions is a tool for social justice storytelling and cultural activism (Krikowa & Aguas, in press). Its use of online platforms for dissemination allows it to

---

**Supplementary Information** The online version contains supplementary material available at https://doi.org/10.1007/978-3-031-77025-8_6. The videos can be accessed individually by clicking on the DOI link above or by scanning this link with the SN More Media App.

bypass traditional media gatekeepers and provides an avenue for counter-hegemonic discourse by minority practitioners. The non-linear format and design of the work disrupts conventional linear narratives and encourages the participatory ethic of fan cultures. Through the digital preservation of the fans' experiences, the project also constitutes a queer "archive of feelings" (Cvetkovich, 2003, p. 7), valorising queer fandom and mitigating the institutional erasure and invisibility of queer lives. As a digital archive, Queer Interruptions inhabits multiple temporalities by bringing the past into the present while negotiating the obsolescence and transience of digital technologies. The non-linear temporalities inherent in the website's video content, navigation, and status as digital storage queer the digital space and speak to the delay, melancholia, and present-pastness of the contemporary queer experience.

The website homepage opens on an animated clock with several hands moving out of sync. To the right, there is explanatory text on the project's context and website navigation instructions. In keeping with the non-normative nature of queer time, the website is laid out in a non-linear fashion allowing viewers to navigate backward, forward, and laterally between videos (Figs. 6.1 and 6.2). The final structure of the online documentary consists of five vignettes, organised by theme: *Queer Interruptions: Delay, Belatedness and Wasted Time*; *Queer Interruptions: Straight Time and Normativity*; *Queer Anachronism: Bury Your Gays and "Feeling Backward"*; *Queer Futures: Potentiality and Unboundedness*; and *"This time doesn't have a place for me"—With Dr. Rebecca Hall*. The vignettes are set out in a clockwise flow, though they can be viewed in any order. A short description of the ideas explored in each vignette is available via a button to the side of each page. The website's background consists of the names of more than 200 lesbian and bisexual female characters killed on television since 1976 (Riese, 2023). The website also incorporates quotes taken from online surveys conducted with participants in the early stages of recruitment. The quotes were selected for their affective qualities and matched to specific videos to complement the themes explored in each.

Katja Lee (2021) explains that within fan studies, there is an ethical imperative to share the results of research with the communities studied as a way to "give back" and participate in the gift economy of fan cultures (p. 3.1). Karen Hellekson (2009) writes that this gift culture is decidedly anti-commercial and centres on exchange: one gives, receives, and reciprocates fan-made creative works without regard for economic profit.

**Fig. 6.1** A screenshot of the Queer Interruptions website showing how the non-linear placement of the videos suggests backward and forward movements through digital space (Aguas, 2021)

Though these fannish gifts lack commercial value, their importance lies in their ability to "create and cement a social structure," thereby fostering solidarity within a fan community (p. 115). Queer Interruptions participates in this gift economy by aligning with and contributing to an online Clexa fan culture characterised by digital fluency, information-sharing, and solidarity.

To "[speak] to the community in its own language" (Lee, 2021, p. 5.6), the online documentary was conceived with a media-savvy and politically inclined Clexa fan community in mind. These fans are predominantly active through online networks such as Tumblr, which Allison McCracken (2017) describes as a "powerful site of youth media literacy, identity formation, and political awareness" for minority groups, including people of colour and LGBTQ+ communities (p. 152). She writes that Tumblr enables the formation of counterpublics for marginalised groups who employ a range of media skills for their social critiques: "creative visual and audio production, fluency in visual

**Fig. 6.2** A screenshot of the Queer Interruptions website showing how the non-linear design can disrupt conventional linear narratives (Aguas, 2021)

culture and remix practices, detailed textual analysis and critical commentary, educational and historical perspectives, [and] personal testimonies" (p. 158). To align the project with the online Clexa fan community's ethos and aesthetics, Queer Interruptions is primarily image-based, utilising streaming video and animation to present the fans' personal testimonies of queerness, ongoing homophobia, and imagined queer futures. It was vital that the work was made available online and not limited by an academic paywall, ensuring accessibility for international fans and those with financial or privacy concerns. To this end, the work deviates from a conventional, linear documentary project and prioritises online delivery, allowing for proximity (or privacy) both temporally and geographically while also providing flexibility in structure and presentation.

As a fan gift, it was imperative that Queer Interruptions was beneficial to, desired, and welcomed by the fandom (Feisler, 2021).[1] The work has received positive feedback from the Clexa fan community, with many fans

[1] Casey Fiesler was speaking at the Fan Studies Ethics Plenary at the 2021 Fan Studies Network North America (FSNNA) Conference.

expressing gratitude for how the project educates the broader community on issues of queer representation. The website also contributes to a fan culture that validates the experiences of queer fans and helps to create a sense of solidarity and support. For example, several queer media websites, LezWatch.TV (Epstein, 2021) and The Geekiary (Wolff, 2021) feature articles on the project with LezWatch.TV writing:

> The thing is... you're not alone. We're not alone. And while we are still struggling to carve space out so all of our stories can be told, if you've ever felt out of step with the world, know you have friends. (Epstein, 2021)

The project's exploration of queer representation and fan experience aligns with an online Clexa fan community centred on "affect, identity, and social justice" (McCracken, 2017, p. 161). Rather than a study that extracts from the community without giving back, the project is an act of reciprocity for the fans' time and labour in completing research surveys and participating in interviews. The website not only appeals to the fans' interest in their chosen media object but also serves to advance the fan community's social and political goals as they campaign for improved queer representation. Queer Interruptions participates in a fannish gift economy by "[making] a gift of my labor, time, and creative energy" (Lee, 2021, p. 4.5).

Drawing on the work of Ann Cvetkovich (2003), the website can also be seen as a queer "archive of feelings," where it acts as a repository of the feelings, ephemera, and textures of queer lives (p. 7). Cvetkovich writes that community grassroots archives fulfil the "emotional need for history" for queer communities whose histories are often suppressed or absent from institutional archives. Alexander Cho (2015) also explains that queer people have "a troubled relationship" with traditional archives that rely on visible and factual records, where "often, queer history can only manifest in what we usually consider secret, ephemeral, or even intuited or felt" (p. 48). Queer Interruptions negotiates the limitations of archives to capture queer ephemera, and the limitations of abstract queer theory to reflect the lived experiences of queer people. In this tenuous position, it was essential that the Queer Interruptions website utilised visual media to capture the intangible, obscure, and inexplicable dimensions of the queer fan experience. The documentary videos serve to illuminate the "idiosyncrasies of emotional life" (Cvetkovich, 2003, p. 6), articulating what resides in the gaps and silences between the abstract and material, the intuited and the factual, the affective and archivable.

As a queer, visual archive of feelings, Queer Interruptions stands as a counterarchive of the intangible and unorthodox, recentring queer histories from the margins. The website is easily distributed, accessible, instantaneous, interactive, and immediate—diverging from conventional institutional archives marked by delay and unidirectional communication. Although the website does not have the search and retrieve function of a traditional archive, it succeeds as a repository of queer feelings through the digital preservation of the fans' testimonials, thereby "turn[ing] what seems like idiosyncratic feeling into historical experience" (Cvetkovich, 2003, p. 166).

Queer Interruptions is also situated within an intrinsically archival fan practice. Arguing that internet fan cultures are archival cultures, Abigail De Kosnik (2016) writes that fans approach "media *as* archive," as raw material to be plundered, expanded upon, and manipulated (p. 11, emphasis in original). Fans then become active archivists, where the mass media archive is seen as "open, capacious, permitting infinite withdrawals and welcoming of an infinite array of additional entrants and entries" (De Kosnik, 2016, p. 279). The unidirectional flow of information in traditional print archives is challenged by fan archival culture, where fans extract, adapt, and add to an unbounded and dynamic mass media archive. De Kosnik writes that for marginalised fans—those that are "nonwhite, nonmale, nonheteronormative" (2016, p. 11)—this archive culture is decidedly political: "to prove to the future that particular queer and female ways of being and making existed" (p. 17). The fans' expansion of the mass media archive and the creation and maintenance of grassroots counter-archives make the community's history legible and transferable, thereby conferring legitimacy and combatting institutional disregard.

Queer Interruptions constitutes my own contribution to the mass media archive and encourages the fan archive impulse. For example, Des (24 years old, White, she/her, demisexual lesbian, Oklahoma, U.S.), a queer Clexa fan, shared her reaction to the website via private correspondence[2] on Tumblr:

---

[2] Additional ethics approval was granted for the use of personal correspondence with respondents in this study, approval number UTS HREC REF NO. ETH21-6591.

I will admit I had to fast forward a little—I still to this day can't watch Lexa's death scene. It triggers and sets me off ... But I love being able to see people talk about their experiences and I think this is so important! I've never made a YouTube video/video blog in my life but I swear this is making me want to, just to participate and share those experiences in case it helps people.

The work compelled Des to further expand on the archive—both the mass media archive and my website-as-archive—and illustrates the generative potential of an unbounded and open fan archive practice. Alana Kumbier (2014) writes that fan cultural production highlights the fans' multiple roles as subcultural participants, archivists, activists, and documentarians: "By empowering members of their subcultures and communities to take on these roles, they create conditions for producing a diverse, inclusive historical record" (p. 196). The website illustrates the participatory ethic of fan archive culture and the multiplicity of roles enacted by fans and myself as a fan and researcher. As a queer, fannish archive of feelings, the project captures the ephemeral and intangible textures of queer fan experience, recuperating the histories of not only marginalised queers but also those of stigmatised fans on the periphery.

Queer Interruptions also fosters the participatory ethic of fan archive culture by allowing viewers to become co-producers of meaning. Building on Henry Jenkins' conception of fans as "active participants in the construction and circulation of textual meanings" (1992, p. 24), the website navigation allows for interactive meaning-making as viewers create their own narrative connections as part of an interpretive fan community. Viewers become users as they make their own path through the documentary videos and interview quotes, viewing them in any order. Leveraging the affordances of new media, the ability of interactive documentaries (i-docs) to "move from passive transmission to collaborative engagement is one of the most interesting aspects of its online manifestation" (Dinmore, 2014, p. 123). As Jon Dovey and Mandy Rose (2013) argue, the meeting of participatory culture and documentary offers users "varying degrees and modes of editorial influence and control," where the text becomes meaningful to the user through this interactivity and the associations they make (p. 370). Queer Interruptions' non-linear spatiotemporal organisation allows for multiple pathways and meanings to be generated. The user's ability to navigate between these vignettes in a non-linear fashion—creating their own narrative connections—distributes authorship and appoints users as co-producers of meaning.

Co-authorship is further negotiated by the user's ability to share the videos to external online platforms. Each video is hosted on Vimeo and can be easily shared or embedded in other websites or social networks, allowing for a degree of meaning-making as users create further narrative, temporal, and spatial connections. However, Dovey and Rose (2013) also point to the tension between the potential for "infinite polyvocality" and editorial control (p. 370). Dividing the more extended vignettes into shorter videos would have increased retention rates, but due to the non-linear navigation, not all the videos would be viewed as intended. While the interactive navigation allows for a degree of co-authorship, this is limited by the need to present each vignette with narrative linearity—a beginning, middle, and end.

In tandem with the fans' testimonials, the website demonstrates how queer temporalities take material form in complex and contradictory ways. As Amy Stone and Jaime Cantrell (2015) assert, "queer lives, often marked by their ephemeral, nonlinear, and nonsequential nature, are contained in archival spaces that are equally textured and complex" (p. 5). The transience of digital media culture, the website's non-linear navigation, and the melancholic video content point to the complex temporalities and textures inherent my website-as-archive.

The ephemerality and transience of digital media render Queer Interruptions a temporally dynamic archival space. Kumbier (2014) writes that archives break down the barriers between past, present, and future, compressing time and space as they "represent and transmit historical and emotional information" (p. 15). However, Wolfgang Ernst (2013) questions the archivability of digital media, which relies on technological continuity. While traditional print archives are associated with the preservation of static objects, the eventual obsolescence of technologies and operating systems render digital archives transient, fleeting, and ephemeral. Wendy Chun (2011) also highlights the illusory stability of digital archive technologies:

> It enables a logic of "permanence" that conflates memory with storage, the ephemeral with the enduring. Through a process of constant regeneration, of constant "reading," it creates an enduring ephemeral that promises to last forever, even as it marches toward obsolescence/stasis. The paradox:

what does not change does not endure, yet change — progress (endless upgrades) — ensures that what endures will fade. (p. 137)

The longevity of Queer Interruptions relies on constancy: of technology, operating platforms, website maintenance, web hosting, and financial investment, all of which will eventually expire. Rather than detracting from its archival aims, the illusory permanence of the website represents its embrace of the tensions and ambivalences of queer temporalities.

Rebecca Coleman (2020) argues that digital culture itself is characterised by temporal flux. She writes that the experience of the internet is multitemporal and paradoxical, marked by a "present temporality of both inertia and movement, continuity and change, the same and the new, difference and repetition" (p. 78). Analysing the temporalities of the "refresh" function, she draws out a sense of repetition and "againness" (p. 77): how "in a 'going forward' there may also be a 'going back,' or a 'being behind' and a sense of the continual looping of temporality; a perpetual starting again" (p. 75). Coleman's sense of backward advances resonates with what Annamarie Jagose (2009) describes as the "back-to-the-future loops" of queer time (p. 158). These rhizomatic digital movements are expressed through the non-linear navigation of the Queer Interruptions website, which evokes a sense of interruption, dislocation, and movement through time and space, immersing the user in temporal fluidity. The user's negotiation of temporal flux—of the enduring ephemerality of the digital archive; the againness of the website refresh; and the non-linearity of the website design—follows a "trajectory that is warped, coiled, broken, and multiple, or at the very least, *not straight*" (Cho, 2015, p. 47, emphasis in original). The overall form and design of my website-as-archive inhabits the liminal, the anomalous, and the disordered. The user experience resists linearity and creates an archival space that speaks to my respondents' deviation from the forward thrust and rigid chronology of heteronormative temporalities.

The fans' melancholic video testimonials also create a digital space to dwell in queer injury. X user, Alice M. Kelly (29 years old, White, she/her, lesbian, U.K.) shared her reaction to the website via private message, where she identified fandom as a site of melancholia:

> You have made me think about how often f/f fandom can be a space of intense pain and grief because it's so rarely about a supportive or inclusive media object, and so frequently about fighting for representation (and

fighting is hard and sometimes we just want nice scenes of people in love eating breakfast food). I think bury your gays is like an indelible part of every lesbian, queer female, genderqueer story because it's more than just an expectation, it's a story structure—it's in the language. There are probably more stories about lesbians where the lesbians die than where they're just okay.

Alice identifies femslash fandom as a space to grieve queer deaths onscreen—the repetitive reminders of their failure to inhabit normative ideals. This ongoing grief renders queer fandom and the Queer Interruptions website as sites of melancholia, where the queer pain of the past stubbornly persists in the present. The website keeps the past alive through "reencounters" and "ongoing reinvestments" with loss (Liu, 2019, p. 189), destabilising the boundaries between the past and present in a temporally fluid archive.

The past-present temporal movements of queer archival spaces are also reflected in the website design and aesthetics. The background comprises the names of more than 200 lesbian and bisexual female characters killed on television since 1976 (Riese, 2023). The fans' testimonials are visually placed among this enduring history of queer death and loss, symbolising their dwelling in the past and the backwardness of queer melancholic temporalities. Several character names have also been transformed into buttons that present emotive quotes taken from online surveys with participants, creating an interface through which the past makes incursions into the present (Fig. 6.3). The buttons utilise a hover or mouseover function rather than a click function to give them a sense of transience and of unexpected reencounters with the past. This sense of haunting resonates with J. E. Muñoz's (1999) assertion that queer melancholia compels us to "take our dead with us to the various battles we must wage in their names—and in our names" (p. 74). The videos and buttons allow the past to reach into the present and reflect the ways queer archival temporalities can "touch across time" (Dinshaw, 1999, p. 21). Positioning these buttons randomly across each screen encourages a "logic of exploration" and "a more active level of engagement" from viewers (Dinmore, 2014, p. 125). Here, the non-linear and fragmented interactivity transforms the symbolic temporal multiplicity of the buttons, quotes, and imagery into an embodied experience of queer time.

The queer temporalities inherent in the design, content, and spatiality of the Queer Interruptions website queer digital space and create a user

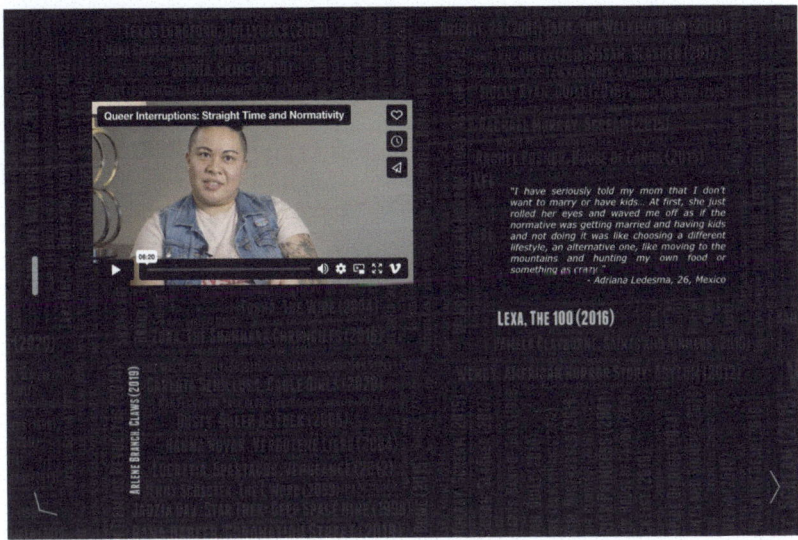

**Fig. 6.3**  A screenshot of the Queer Interruptions website showing the hover buttons that present quotes from respondents' online surveys (Aguas, 2021)

experience marked by temporal fluidity. In her analysis of the Lesbian Herstory Archives (LHA) in New York, Agatha Beins (2015) draws attention to how the spatial configuration of an archive shapes the user's "affective experience" (p. 32). She writes:

> How does a person's body fit into the archives and how does that affect what a visitor feels in the archives? How are our identities reflected in and created by the archive? These questions are not just intellectual but political, and they are not only about an archive's content but also about how the space of an archive is curated. (p. 26)

Drawing on the work of Sara Ahmed, Beins describes how the heterosexualisation of social space and the failure of queer bodies to adhere to norms results in an experience of queer discomfort. For Queer Interruptions users, this discomfort is expressed as a feeling of displacement—of fluidity, liminality, againstness, and melancholic backwardness. The multitemporalities of the website design, content, and non-linear navigation speak to the discomfort and displacement of queerness within heteronormativity.

Rather than being paralysing or distressing, Ahmed (2004) argues that this sense of displacement is productive:

> Discomfort is hence not about assimilation or resistance, but about inhabiting norms differently. The inhabitance is generative or productive insofar as it does not end with the failure of norms to be secured, but with possibilities of living that do not "follow" those norms through. (p. 155, emphasis in original)

When my respondents describe their ideal queer futures—involving partner/s, animals, and queered family units with or without children—they are embracing the discomfort of deviating from heteronormativities. In this spatial and temporal unknown, my respondents can envision new temporalities and ways of living, an openness that resonates with J. E. Muñoz's (2009) conception of a queer futurity characterised by potentiality and unboundedness. The website's embrace of displacement and its possibilities results in a digital queer archive of feelings, where trauma, melancholy, and bad feelings are "provocation[s] to create alternative life worlds" (Cvetkovich, 2003, p. 237). The spatiality of the website reflects the experience of queer discomfort within heteronormativity and illustrates the alternative queer chronologies and unbounded ways of being that are made possible through this displacement.

To view the related documentary video on your device, please click on the DOI link provided under the Supplementary Information section of this chapter or scan the link with the SN More Media App (Fig. 6.4).

## QUEER TEMPORALITIES, EMBODIED

Through its multitemporal form and content, the online documentary, Queer Interruptions is an effective vehicle to express the complex abstractions of queer time and its intersections with fan experience, archive culture, and digital media. Its use of visual media captures the gestural, intangible, and inexplicable elements of the fans' emotional lives, uncovering the gaps and (dis)harmonies between the abstract and the material; the ephemeral and the archivable. As an interactive online documentary, Queer Interruptions disseminates the research beyond academic and mainstream media institutions, allowing it to effectively engage with counterpublics. Its visual form also aligns with a media-savvy and politically engaged online fan community, appealing to their ethos of diversity,

**Fig. 6.4** A screenshot from *Queer Futures: Potentiality and Unboundedness* (Aguas, 2021)

education, and social justice. As a fan gift, the website reciprocates fan labour spent participating in the research by advancing the fan community's goals and contributing to a fan culture of solidarity-building and support.

As a digital archive of feelings, Queer Interruptions is a recuperative project that combats the institutional silence, erasure, and invisibility of queer lives. However, the illusory permanence of digital culture renders it transient and fleeting. Rather than limiting its archival aims, this digital transience is embraced as a further expression of the ambivalent and paradoxical temporalities of queer time. The fans' experiences of displacement, ephemerality, non-linearity, and melancholic backwardness are preserved in an equally dynamic archival space. Through its design, content, and status as digital storage, Queer Interruptions speaks to my respondents' deviations from the forward, linear thrust of heteronormative chronologies as it places queer temporalities in dialogue with lived experience.

# REFERENCES

Aguas, E. (2021, July). *Queer Interruptions*. https://queerinterruptions.com
Ahmed, S. (2004). *The cultural politics of emotion*. Routledge.
Balsamo, A. (2011). *Designing culture: The technological imagination at work*. Duke University Press.
Beins, A. (2015). Making a place for lesbian life at the Lesbian Herstory Archives. In A. L. Stone & J. Cantrell (Eds.), *Out of the closet, into the archives: Researching sexual histories* (pp. 25–49). State University of New York Press.
Cho, A. (2015). Queer reverb: Tumblr, affect, time. In K. Hillis, S. Paasonen & M. Petit (Eds.), *Networked affect* (pp. 43–57). The MIT Press. https://doi.org/10.7551/mitpress/9715.001.0001
Chun, W. H. K. (2011). *Programmed visions: Software and memory*. The MIT Press.
Coleman, R. (2020). Refresh: On the temporalities of digital media "re's." *Media Theory, 4*(2), 55–84.
Cvetkovich, A. (2003). An archive of feelings: Trauma, sexuality, and lesbian public cultures. *Duke University Press*. https://doi.org/10.1215/9780822238 4434
De Kosnik, A. (2016). Rogue archives: Digital cultural memory and media fandom. *MIT Press*. https://doi.org/10.7551/mitpress/10248.001.0001
Dinmore, S. (2014). The real online: Database documentary and knowledge space. *Journal of Media Practice, 15*(2), 123–132. https://doi.org/10.1080/14682753.2014.960765
Dinshaw, C. (1999). *Getting medieval: Sexualities and communities, pre- and postmodern*. Duke University Press. https://doi.org/10.17077/1536-8742.1471
Dovey, J., & Rose, M. (2013). "This great mapping of ourselves": New documentary forms online. In B. Winston (Ed.), *The documentary film book* (pp. 366–375). Palgrave Macmillan. https://doi.org/10.1007/978-1-349-92625-1_41
Epstein, M. A. (2021, August 18). *PhDs, queerbaiting, and Queer Interruptions*. LezWatch.TV. https://lezwatchtv.com/2021/phds-queerbaiting-and-queer-interruptions
Ernst, W. (2013). *Digital memory and the archive*. University of Minnesota Press.
Hellekson, K. (2009). A fannish field of value: Online fan gift culture. *Cinema Journal, 48*(4), 113–118. https://doi.org/10.1353/cj.0.0140
Jagose, A. (2009). Feminism's queer theory. *Feminism & Psychology, 19*(2), 157–174.
Jenkins, H. (1992). Textual poachers: Television fans and participatory culture. *Routledge*. https://doi.org/10.4324/9780203114339

Krikowa, N., & Aguas, E. (in press). Documenting diversity on screen: Interactive documentaries (i-docs) as tools for queer advocacy. *Media Practice and Education.*

Kumbier, A. (2014). *Ephemeral material: Queering the archive.* Litwin Books.

Lee, K. (2021). Acafan methodologies and giving back to the fan community. *Transformative Works and Cultures, 36.* https://doi.org/10.3983/twc.2021. 2025

Liu, W. (2019). Narrating against assimilation and the empire: Diasporic mourning and queer Asian melancholia. *WSQ: Women's Studies Quarterly, 47*(1), 176–192. https://doi.org/10.1353/wsq.2019.0020

McCracken, A. (2017). Tumblr youth subcultures and media engagement. *Cinema Journal, 1,* 151–161. https://doi.org/10.1353/cj.2017.0061

Muñoz, J. E. (1999). *Disidentifications: Queers of color and the performance of politics.* University of Minnesota Press.

Riese. (2023, February 27). All 235 dead lesbian and bisexual characters on TV, and how they died. *Autostraddle.* Retrieved November 18, 2023, from https://www.autostraddle.com/all-65-dead-lesbian-and-bisexual-characters-on-tv-and-how-they-died-312315/

Stone, A. L., & Cantrell, J. (2015). Introduction: Something queer at the archive. In A.L. Stone & J. Cantrell (Eds.), *Out of the closet, into the archives: Researching sexual histories* (pp. 1–24). State University of New York Press. https://doi.org/10.31274/archivalissues.11036

Wolff, J. (2021, July 17). "Queer Interruptions" examines impact of "Bury Your Gays". The Geekiary. https://thegeekiary.com/queer-interruptions-examines-impact-of-bury-your-gays/98607

# CHAPTER 7

# Life After Death (on Repeat)

On 10th April 2022, fans, once again, found themselves subject to the anachronistic turns of queer time. The series finale for the popular Emmy Award-winning drama, *Killing Eve* (Morris et al., 2018–2022) ended with the death of the queer female assassin, Villanelle. Just minutes beforehand, she had finally consummated a four-season-long mutual obsession with the other lead female character, Eve.

Echoing Lexa's death six years earlier, mainstream media called attention to the show's use of the "Bury Your Gays" trope, with *Variety* chief TV critic Caroline Framke writing, "anyone who's gotten invested in a TV love story between two queer women should've been steeling themselves for tragedy the second Eve and Villanelle finally found some semblance of happiness" (2022).[1] Criticism of the finale also centred on the writers' careless disdain for the show's sizeable queer fan base in knowingly employing the trope amid renewed anti-LGBTQ+ legislation and attacks on transgender people in the United States. Writing for *CNN*, A. J. Willingham (2022) stated:

---

[1] See also: "How *Killing Eve's* finale betrayed its queer community," *Refinery29* (Bashforth, 2022); "*Killing Eve* chose cruelty," *Vulture* (Bastién, 2022); "*Killing Eve* just ended in the worst possible way," *Digital Spy* (Opie, 2022); "The *Killing Eve* finale has infuriated queer fans," *Junkee* (Salem, 2022); "*Killing Eve* fans hated the finale—but they're taking the final word for themselves," *Vanity Fair* (Still, 2022); "*Killing Eve* just aired the worst TV series finale since *Game of Thrones*," *Inverse* (Welch, 2022).

E. Aguas, *Queer Interruptions*, Palgrave Fan Studies, https://doi.org/10.1007/978-3-031-77025-8_7

Fiction can shape the future, and every time a popular queer character is eliminated in a way that feels inexorably tied to their queerness (even if they are a murderous psychopath), it echoes the dangerous promises of systemic prejudice and oppression. If the people who create our fiction can't imagine a world beyond that, then what chance does reality have?

Devasted fans drew parallels between the two deaths, where both were shot mere moments after consummating their respective romantic relationships, and where showrunners had actively courted queer audiences:

Villanelle's death brought back the same pain that Lexa left behind. Ultimately, the show repeated the familiar pattern of gathering an LGBTQ+ fanbase — one that frankly kept the show going for so long — ripping all the joy right from under them, and robbing Eve and Villanelle of their joy, too. (Clements, 2022)

The fans' reactions mirror those of my respondents, where Villanelle's onscreen death caused them to relive the queer pain of the past and how, for respondent Elizabeth Bridges, the shattering of illusions of progress was "like the rug getting ripped out from under you." Villanelle's death was not only a reiteration of the long history of queer female character death but also a reiteration of the queer (fan) temporalities explored in this study. These self-referential loops speak to the anachronistic and melancholic untimeliness of queer fan experience, whose perpetual backwardness highlights the continuing relevance of this research.

In keeping with the non-linear nature of queer time, I'd like to turn backward and return to my opening quote (Fig. 7.1).

This book and the accompanying online documentary have explored what these time-travelling wounds look like for queer fans: how could Lexa's death transport fans backward to painful memories? What does it mean to "feel backward" while "looking forward" (Love, 2007, p. 27)? How do delay, belatedness, and anachronism manifest in their lived experience? By framing the fans' experiences as queer temporal movements, we can identify persistent blurrings and repetitive oscillations between past and present; visibility and erasure; assimilation and alienation; dissidence and depoliticisation. Their testimonials highlight the different facets of queer temporalities in the fans' emotional and material realities, providing us with a more nuanced view of the passage of progress and allowing us to question the extent of liberation.

**Heather Hogan** ✔
@theheatherhogan

Follow ⌄

## Straight TV writers will never understand how they can inflict time-traveling wounds that hurt us as scared gay children all over again.

9:57 AM - 4 Mar 2016

**Fig. 7.1** A post on X by fan and media critic, Heather Hogan after Lexa's death in *The 100* (Hogan, 2016; Morgenstein & Rothenberg, 2014–2020)

Against the "placating propaganda" of queer liberation (Schulman, 2012, p. 66), this research has shown how prevailing heterotemporalities continue to marginalise and oppress queer communities. The fans' feelings of delay and belatedness point to the pervasive straight time logics and chrononormativities that cast them as unproductive and devalued, robbing them of time, opportunity, health, and happiness. Their persistent bad feelings and melancholia draw out the continuities between a homophobic bad gay past and our liberatory present. For racialised queer female sexualities under White supremacy, this melancholic backwardness fosters an intimacy with the suffering of the colonial past—a transgenerational haunting that highlights the similar logics of control spanning communities and generations. In this context, the seemingly trivial repetition of a queer female character's death speaks to the very real trauma of living in a world that continues to be inhospitable for queer people and queer people of colour.

While delay and belatedness often bear negative connotations, several of my respondents frame temporal deviation as beneficial and necessary. Biggs and Daatland (2006) argue that there is a need to recognise the "positive value of discontinuity" (p. 5), where my respondents' deliberate stasis ensured their safety—"I knew I was not straight, but I wasn't going to do anything about it, for survival"—and which allowed them to explore their sexuality later in life with greater freedom and independence. Rather than engendering a sense of shame, their embrace of discontinuity actualised alternative queer adulthoods where a good life is not tethered to expectations of marriage and sexual and economic (re)productivity.

The fans' experiences also illustrate the political potential of bad, backward feelings where, rather than being paralysed with hopelessness, the fans' melancholia is generative—raising significant funds for an LGBTQ+ charity, inspiring the donation of hundreds of queer fiction books and fuelling activism calling for improved queer representation. The fans' responses demonstrate that melancholia is not a self-indulgent negative affect but the catalyst for meaningful social action and political change.

My own bad feelings of anger, sadness, and hopelessness after Lexa's death motivated this research and the creation of the Queer Interruptions (Aguas, 2021) online documentary. The digital preservation of the fans' bad feelings and melancholia renders the website a queer archive of feelings, recuperating the histories of queer female and genderqueer fans and shifting these communities from the margins of predominately White, male, straight, and cisgender bodies of scholarship. The positive reception from fans is evidence of its reparative work as a fan gift, validating the fans' experiences and transmitting these histories to the future. As an exploration of abstract queer theory and its expression in lived experience, the website relies on documentary video to capture the intricacies of emotional life, positioning it as a paradoxical visual archive of the elusive and transient. Through its video content, website design, and its status as digital storage, the work embraces the contradictions, ephemerality, and fluidity of queer temporalities.

While this research brings marginalised fans from the periphery to the centre, I acknowledge its limitations in amplifying those voices. All participants were English-speaking, with the majority identifying as abled and cisgender, though several participants came out as genderqueer over the course of the work. Western media (specifically North American media) also features prominently in this research. While I have included the responses of several genderqueer participants, the analysis does not delve into the nuances of non-normative genders and temporality. Further research on gender-diverse fans would combat their continuing invisibility and elucidate the unique temporal contours of transgender, non-binary, and genderqueer lives. More work also needs to be done to decolonise fan studies. The dominant Whiteness of the field, fan communities, and media objects requires collective reflexivity and the amplification of under-represented voices. My hope is for this research to spur further discussion on non-Western, marginalised queer fans while retaining a queer ethos to disrupt sexual and gender binaries, emphasising ambiguity, fluidity, and indefinability.

With increasing queer representation onscreen and the continued use of the Bury Your Gays trope—and its more recent evolution into "Cancel Your Gays"—queer audiences are left to navigate between visibility and erasure; acceptance and exclusion. As long as White heteronormativity continues to structure everyday life—of which queer death onscreen is a symptom—queer fans will continue to grapple with the temporal oscillations of marginality. Their backward-forward, past-present movements render them outside of chronology: the *elsewhere* of belatedness and the *nowhere* of unresolved assimilation. However, embracing this displacement offers visions of queer potentiality and "an excitement in the face of the uncertainty of where the discomfort may take us" (Ahmed, 2004, p. 155). As my respondent, Rebecca Hall (55), so aptly expresses:

> The present is impossible. The past is horrific. So, you know, where to inhabit? I think it involves going back and forward, back in time, forward in time, trying to re-vision and re-imagine the world around us. And I think it's also the most radical thing we can do because we've got to have an understanding of what a liveable future looks like in order to create it.

The fans' fluidities and temporal fluctuations displace dominant heterotemporalities, allowing new and divergent temporal orders to materialise. In the fans' experiences of "feeling backward" while "looking forward" (Love, 2007, p. 27), there is not only an acknowledgement of the queer pain of the past and the inadequacies of the present but also an imperative to utilise these bad feelings to displace the *elsewhere* and *nowhere* with a better, queerer, more liveable future.

## REFERENCES

Aguas, E. (2021, July). *Queer Interruptions*. https://queerinterruptions.com

Ahmed, S. (2004). *The cultural politics of emotion*. Routledge.

Bashforth, E. (2022, April 12). How *Killing Eve*'s finale betrayed its queer community. *Refinery29*. https://www.refinery29.com/en-au/killing-eve-season-4-finale-betrayed-queer-narrative

Bastién, A. J. (2022, April 16). *Killing Eve* chose cruelty. *Vulture*. https://www.vulture.com/2022/04/the-ending-of-killing-eve-season-4-explained.html

Biggs, S., & Daatland, S. O. (2006). Ageing and diversity: A critical introduction. In S. O. Daatland & S. Biggs (Eds.), *Ageing and diversity: Multiple pathways and cultural migrations* (pp. 1–12). The Policy Press. https://doi.org/10.51952/9781447366560

Clements, S. (2022, April 11). As a queer *Killing Eve* fan, I feel betrayed. *Them.* https://www.them.us/story/killing-eve-finale-queer-fans

Framke, C. (2022, April 10). Killing Eve ends with a total betrayal of what once made it great (SPOILERS). *Variety.* https://variety.com/2022/tv/reviews/killing-eve-finale-review-villanelle-dies-1235226751/

Hogan, H. [@theheatherhogan]. (2016, March 4). *Straight TV writers will never understand how they can inflict time-traveling wounds that hurt us as scared gay children all.* X. https://web.archive.org/web/20190727050802/https://twitter.com/theheatherhogan/status/705814487786512384

Love, H. (2007). *Feeling backward: Loss and the politics of queer history.* Harvard University Press.

Morgenstein, L., & Rothenberg, J. (Executive Producers). (2014–2020). *The 100* [TV series]. Alloy Entertainment; CBS Television Studios; Warner Bros. Television.

Morris, L., Oh, S., Waller-Bridge P., Gentle, S. W., Mingacci, G., & Thomas, D. (Executive Producers). (2018–2022). *Killing Eve* [TV series]. BBC America; Endeavour Content; Sid Gentle Films.

Opie, D. (2022, April 11). *Killing Eve just ended in the worst possible way.* Digital Spy. https://www.digitalspy.com/tv/a39626218/killing-eve-season-4-ending-explained-death/

Salem, M. (2022, April 12). *The Killing Eve finale has infuriated queer fans.* Junkee. https://junkee.com/killing-eve-finale-homophic/327483

Schulman, S. (2012). *The gentrification of the mind: Witness to a lost imagination.* University of California Press.

Still, J. (2022, April 13). *Killing Eve Fans hated the finale—But they're taking the final word for themselves. Vanity Fair.* https://www.vanityfair.com/hollywood/2022/04/killing-eve-finale-backlash

Willingham, A. J. (2022, April 21). *The harmful trope that's still haunting queer TV.* CNN. https://edition.cnn.com/2022/04/21/entertainment/bury-your-gays-killing-eve-lgbt-trope-cec/index.html

Welch, A. (2022, April 12). *"Killing Eve" just aired the worst TV series finale since "Game of Thrones".* Inverse. https://www.inverse.com/entertainment/killing-eve-series-finale-ending-backlash-explained

# Appendix

## Online Documentary Production

All interviews were filmed in 4K on a Canon XC-15, with footage delivered in HD. Shooting in 4K and finishing in a smaller format allowed me to use a single camera and punch in for interview close-ups during post-production. I used a three-point lighting set-up and had a maximum of two crew members to assist with sound monitoring and set-up.

The documentary assets were edited using Premiere Pro, and preliminary edits were presented at conferences to gather viewer feedback. I performed all post-production, including grading and audio editing.

The online documentary website was built using Hype, which allowed me to create the backward-forward and lateral navigation required without high-level coding. Each video is also accessible through the Vimeo website. The design and aesthetics of the online documentary are discussed in more detail in Chapter 6, "Queer Interruptions: A Fan Gift and Queer Archive of Feelings."

# INDEX

The manufacturer's authorised representative in the EU is Springer
Nature Customer Service Centre GmbH, Europaplatz 3, 69115 Heidelberg,
Germany. If you have any concerns regarding our products, please
contact ProductSafety@springernature.com

Printed and bound by CPI Group (UK) Ltd, Croydon, CR0 4YY
29/04/2026
02099471-0014